HYDROPONICS

Beginner's Guide to Quickly Start Growing Your Own Vegetables, Fruits, & Herbs and Learn How to Build Your Own Hydroponics Home Gardening System

By
Rachel Martin

© Copyright 2019 by Rachel Martin - All rights reserved.

This content is provided with the sole purpose of providing relevant information on a specific topic for which every reasonable effort has been made to ensure that it is both accurate and reasonable. Nevertheless, by purchasing this content, you consent to the fact that the author, as well as the publisher, are in no way experts on the topics contained herein, regardless of any claims as such that may be made within. As such, any suggestions or recommendations that are made within are done so purely for entertainment value. It is recommended that you always consult a professional prior to undertaking any of the advice or techniques discussed within.

This is a legally binding declaration that is considered both valid and fair by both the Committee of Publishers Association and the American Bar Association and should be considered as legally binding within the United States.

The reproduction, transmission, and duplication of any of the content found herein, including any specific or extended information will be done as an illegal act regardless of the end form the information ultimately takes. This includes copied versions of the work both physical, digital and audio unless express consent of the Publisher is provided beforehand. Any additional rights reserved.

Furthermore, the information that can be found within the pages described forthwith shall be considered both accurate and truthful when it comes to the recounting of facts. As such, any use, correct or incorrect, of the provided information will render the Publisher free of responsibility as to the actions taken outside of their direct purview. Regardless, there are zero scenarios where the original author or the Publisher can be deemed liable in any fashion for any damages or hardships that may result from any of the information discussed herein.

Additionally, the information in the following pages is intended only for informational purposes and should thus be thought of as universal. As befitting its nature, it is presented without assurance regarding its prolonged validity or interim quality. Trademarks that are mentioned are done without written consent and can in no way be considered an endorsement from the trademark holder.

TABLE OF CONTENTS

Introduction 1
Chapter 1 *What Is Hydroponics?* 3
   Hydroponics 3
   Why Hydroponics? 5
   Hydroponics Will Soon Take the Bulk of Agricultural Production
   6
   How Hydroponics Works 7
   Is It Hard? 8
   Crops You Could Grow 9
   The Growing Systems 10
   Pipes and Troughs 10
   Stones or Sand Culture 11
   Beds 11
   Trays 11
   Bags 12
Chapter 2 *Must Have Tools* 13
   A Reservoir 13
   A Growing Chamber 14
   Delivery System 14
   Submersible Pump 15
   Air Pump 15
   Timer 16
   Growing Medium 17
   Growing Lights 17
   PH Testing Kit 18
   The Nutrient Solution 19
   The Quality of the Water Used 20
   The Conditions of the Room 20

A Greenhouse 21

Considerations to Make When Purchasing Hydroponic Tools and Equipment 21

Chapter 3 *Types Of Hydroponic Systems* 25

Aeroponics 25

Nutrient Film Technique (N.F.T.) 26

The Ebb and Flow Hydroponics System 28

Drip Irrigation System 30

The Wick System 31

The Deep-Water Culture System 33

The Kratky Method 34

Fogponics 35

The Dutch Bucket System 36

Chapter 4 *Advantages and Disadvantages of Hydroponics* 39

The Yields Are Higher 39

Plants Grow Quicker 39

Does Not Require a Yard 40

Saves Water 40

Production Can Be Done All-Year-Round 40

Requires Less Labor 41

Does Not Require Any Soil 41

Requires Less Space 41

Less Wastage 42

Produces Higher Quality Yields 42

Hydroponics Farming Is Eco-Friendly 42

Farmers Do Not Have to Deal with Eutrophication When They Take Up Hydroponics 42

Farmers Do Not Have to Deal with Soil Pests and Diseases 43

Hydroponics Makes Agriculture Feasible in Areas That Are Not Naturally Suited to Farming 43

Hydroponics Reduce the Need to Transport Food Items 44

Monoculture Is Allowed 44
There Are No Weeds 44
It Is Easy to Maintain Hydroponic Systems 45
Easier to Control the Costs of Farming 45
Ph Control 45
Hydroponics Is Fun and Makes for an Interesting Hobby 45
Disadvantages of Hydroponics 45
There Are Risks Related to Electricity and Water 46
The Initial Expenses Are Quite High 46
The Costs of Running Are Also Quite High 46
It Takes a While for You to Get a Return on Your Investment .47
Diseases and Pests Spread Quickly 47
Threats of System Failure 48
The Organic Question 48
Requires a Heavy Investment of Time and Commitment 49
Hydroponics Limit Agricultural Production 49
The Entire Hydroponic System Is Quite Vulnerable 50
Requires Some Knowledge and Expertise 50

Chapter 5 *Getting Your Feet Wet* 52
Ensuring That Your Water Will Not Kill Your Plants 55
Beginners Should Opt for Clones 57
Preparing the Growing Media 57
Coming Up with the Correct Watering Cycle for Your Plants .. 58
The Right Nutrition for Hydroponics 59
Why Your Attention Should Remain with the Roots 60
How Does A Good Hydroponics System Look Like? 61
The Best Low-Cost and Environmental-Friendly Way to Power Your Hydroponics System 62

Chapter 6 *Common Mistakes Hydroponics Beginners Make* 65

Chapter 7 *Useful Tips for Hydroponic Farming* 77

Chapter 8 *New Developments in Hydroponics Gardening* 89

New Developments in Lighting 89
Improvements Made on the Hydroponic Nutrients 90
The Rise of Micro Growing of Microgreens............................. 90
Increased Vertical Growing 90
Combination of Aeroponics and Hydroponics......................... 91
Combination of Hydroponics and Soil Gardening....................92
The Advantages 93
Changes in the Sphere of Commercial Hydroponics 93
Advances through Aquaponics and Other Systems 94
Hydroponics in Grocery Stores and Restaurants......................94
Transitioning to the Organic Side...95
Increased Conservation and Sustainability Measures 95
Hydroponics as Part of the Home Décor...................................96
Hydroponics as The Means to Enhance Breathing Air 96
The Hydroponics Carnival Ride 97
Growing Marijuana..97
Into the Future 98
In summary...99
Conclusion 101
Description 102

INTRODUCTION

Congratulations on purchasing *Hydroponics: Beginner's Guide to Quickly Start Growing Your Own Vegetables, Fruits, & Herbs, And Learn How to Build Your Own Hydroponics Home Gardening System,* and thank you for doing so. Hydroponics is increasingly being taken up the choice farming method, and by purchasing this book, you will get to know why hydroponics is becoming so popular, and what you need to do to get a piece of the action too.

Hydroponics is thought to be the bedrock of food security in the future. Crops are not planted in the soil, and instead, inert growing mediums are used to provide support. Since the plants are grown indoors, the farmer is in control of all growing conditions including the nutrients available to the plant. The result is an increased growth rate, increased yields, continuous production, and other benefits, as compared to conventional farming.

Seeing these benefits, big farms and individual farmers are moving in to cash in on these perks. Restaurants and grocery stores are also taking up hydroponics as a way to provide consumers with fresh food or produce, and in the process, beating the competition. The good thing about hydroponics is that it does not restrict in terms of scale; you could grow one plant or thousands of them; it all depends on you.

To that end, the following chapters will discuss hydroponics in detail, explaining to you what exactly hydroponics gardening is, how it works, what you need to have and the crops that can be grown this way. You will also get to know its various tools and equipment you need to assemble for your garden. Hydroponic plants are grown in systems, and this book will let you in on various kinds of hydroponic systems, including the advantages and disadvantages of each. There is so much more to learn from this book; it is hoped that it will be an interesting, yet informative read that will get you situated and ready to hitch the fun and rewarding hydroponics bandwagon.

There are plenty of books on this subject on the market, thanks again for choosing this one! Every effort was made to ensure it is full of as much useful information as possible. Please enjoy!

CHAPTER 1
What Is Hydroponics?

My experience growing flowers and vegetables added to the knowledge I derived from my science classes tells me that one of the most critical constituents for anyone who wants to plant something is soil. It is in the soil that you place the plant for support, apply fertilizer and pour the water that the plant needs. However, as science and technology would have it, soil is not a critical element; a plant just needs a place to anchor its roots and a supply of all the nutrients it would have absorbed from the soil. This is the bedrock of hydroponics.

Hydroponics

Hydroponics is the method of growing crops without soil but providing all the necessary mineral nutrients. A gardener who takes up hydroponics takes on the responsibility of regulating the nutrients composition in the liquid solution he or she prepares for watering the plants. The gardener must also regulate the frequency of this nutrients supply. In other words, the gardener takes the responsibility of regulating the growing environment of the crops. The good thing is that the entire growing process is highly automated, but it still requires a great deal of up-close management.

Although the hydroponics idea sounds like something drawn from a science-fiction movie, it is not new. The Aztecs had created floating farms around Tenochtitlan, their island city, and Marco Polo recorded having seen some floating gardens in some of his travels as he toured China during the 13th century. In addition, as early as the 1930s, Pan American Airways had built a hydroponic farm on a remote island in the Pacific, which would allow its flights to replenish their food supplies en route to Asia. Today, the use of hydroponics is becoming increasingly popular particularly as a way of handling the food demands of the future.

Hydroponics is preferred because it utilizes water and nutrients efficiently mainly because both are applied directly to the roots of the plant. The water and nutrients are primarily responsible for the plant's growth. However, their levels need to be controlled, not just managed, so that the nutrients and water levels can be provided at the required levels.

The availability of lighting is also an important component in crop production. Adequate lighting is achieved by planting the crops in vertical structures so that the crop's accessibility to light is maximized while the crowding, density, and shading are kept at a minimum. In the present day, hydroponic farming has now taken up 3D planting where the plants are grown vertically, and in multilevel beds.

So far, we have seen how hydroponics provides the ideal growing conditions for growing plants, in terms of water, nutrients, and light. These conditions are ideal for crops and will maximize the utility of the growing area, and use the space that could otherwise have been unused. Having a movable multilevel growing structure exposes plants to ideal lighting at all times, during the growing period.

Mainly, hydroponics is used as a controlled agriculture system for growing out of season crops, for producing crops in areas that are less suited for growing crops, and in areas where the water supply cannot support conventional farming. Research centers also take up hydroponics to grow crops they need to study plant nutrition, plant breeding, and plant diseases because the conditions under which the crops are grown can be regulated as desired. Almost all plants can be grown using hydroponics.

When crops are grown in this way, they use up 50% less land and 90% less water when contrasted with traditional crop growing methods. However, the yields from the crops are 4 times more, and the crop growth rate is twice as fast when using hydroponics. This is possible because the crops have everything they would need, at the right concentrations.

In place of the soil used in typical agriculture, the farmer or gardener roots the plants in compounds like vermiculite, clay pellets or rock wool. All substances used must be inert so that they do not introduce any new elements into the plant's environment.

The solution of water and nutrients is then poured over the support material so that the plant can feed into it.

One primary advantage that hydroponics offer over traditional crop husbandry methods is that when the systems are carefully manipulated and the growing environment properly managed, in terms of the quantity of water provided, pH levels and the combination and concentration of the nutrients. When these conditions are looked into carefully, the crops grow faster. There is less waste in regards to the consumption of resources. There is also less reliance on fertilizers, pesticides and other potentially harmful products used in conventional agriculture.

Why Hydroponics?

As the world population has been expanding, there has been an increased need to produce more food, which led to the development of modern industrialized farming. Modern agriculture has lived up to its promise of increased production because there has been a greater supply of fresh, cheap and nutritious food compared to the past, and its effects have particularly been felt in the developed world. However, modern farming has also brought with it challenges such as the promotion of waste, pollution and increased strain on resources.

The development of hydroponics has not only been a response to the current food and resource problems. It is a solution for the future too. Experts say that by 2050, about 80% of all the food produced will be consumed in the cities, which makes it important for the cities to become producers of food. Currently, most cities are the good 'black holes' because all they do is suck in much of it, and at the same time, the cities are the biggest food wasters.

It is easy to see the wastefulness and excessive nature of normal food production in comparison to hydroponics. To supply food to the urban areas, producers need to produce it in large amounts and to transport it there, sometimes, across vast distances, before it is introduced into the market. From the initial step of production, harvesting, packaging, and shipping, the food takes up large amounts of resources that could be saved and re-used elsewhere.

People are involved, pollution-causing fuels, buildings, and other resources, and this is wasteful, in comparison to what hydroponics entails.

As the world's population is getting close to 7.5 billion and the demand for more food increasing just as fast, with emphasis on resource-intensive foods, it is clear that farming needs to be done even in the cities, and even so, more productively.

Hydroponics Will Soon Take the Bulk of Agricultural Production

Although the vast majority of plants are grown using soil, the use of hydroponics has been rising. Thanet Earth, the largest greenhouse complex in the United Kingdom, took up controlled-environment agriculture to produce approximately 225 million tomato fruits, 16 million peppers and 13 million cucumbers in 2013. This production was 12, 11 and 8 percent of Britain's total annual production of these crops, respectively. Thanet Earth made this record-breaking production with only four greenhouses and was hoping to add to this number.

In 2015, it was estimated that hydroponic farming has grown, and was worth $21.4 billion, with an expected annual growth of 7%. It would seem that hydroponics farming is changing slowly, but steadily.

Besides the changing dynamics of farming itself, other outside forces are pushing for the change, advocating for more controlled-agriculture, to boost food production. The earth's population is one key factor. It is expected that by 2050, the global population will have risen by a staggering 3billion persons, and more than 80 percent of the total population will be dwelling in the urban centers. Since we are already using the available farming areas, the arid regions too will need to be converted to production centers, and the way to do this is by introducing hydroponic farming in these areas.

One of the more popular methods is vertical urban farming where hydroponic farms are stacked one over another, in buildings, even in tall skyscrapers. This would be an ideal solution, especially when much of the land is taken up to house the large urban population. It would also place the farms strategically, right where the fresh produce is needed. Singapore and Michigan are already constructing these vertical gardens, and south London is also placing the disused bomb shelters into good use.

Interestingly, as man ventures further and further away from the Earth, NASA is looking into creating hydroponic farms in space to feed the astronauts. The research has been taking place at the University of Arizona, where scientists are looking into the possibility of creating a closed-loop system that will feel carbon dioxide and human waste into a hydroponic farm, which will possibly lead to the creation of oxygen, food, and water.

You could look forward to seeing some space-grown tomatoes in the future, but good luck with the human waste growing material.

How Hydroponics Works

We have already established that in contrast to traditional agriculture where the soil provides support to the plant, allowing it to remain upright and providing a supply of nutrients, in hydroponics plants have artificial support and a solution containing all the required nutrients is provided. The idea behind the hydroponic setup is simple. It is thought that environmental factors often limit plant growth, and therefore, by providing a solution that contains nutrients to the plant's roots, the gardener provides a constant optimal supply of nutrients and water. The nutritional efficiency makes a plant live up to its potential by making it more productive.

The nutrient-rich solution is delivered in a number of ways:

- In the first, the plants are placed in an inert substance, as mentioned earlier, and its roots are occasionally flooded with the solution.

- Secondly, the plants could be placed on the inert substances and the solution rained on the plant using a solution dripper.

- The third option places the plants on a film that slightly slopes, and this allows the solution to trickle down to the roots of the plants
- The fourth way has the plant and its roots suspended in the air, and the roots are occasionally sprayed with the solution mist.

All the methods described above use machines to do one thing or another, either by the use of a mister, or using a pump to deliver the solution from its storage area. The solution must also be aerated so that the roots get the oxygen they require once the solution comes on. Plants need energy to absorb the minerals in the solution, and this absorption process requires energy, which is made possible by respiration.

Is It Hard?

Certainly, setting up and maintaining a hydroponics system can be quite a difficult task. This is because the plants need an assortment of nutrients, and each species' optimal amount of nutrients varies. In addition, each plant's nutritional requirements will change as it goes through various developmental stages. Local conditions such as the hardness of the water to be used also matters a lot.

It is also a fact that some nutrients are absorbed into the plant much faster than others which can cause a buildup of some ions in the solution, hence a change of the solution's pH. Once the pH is affected, the absorption of other nutrients by the plant is hindered because the uptake of some nutrients is pH-dependent, and because the excess availability of some nutrients prevents the uptake of others. For example, when the ammonia content is very high, the calcium uptake decreases, and on the other hand, too much calcium reduces the absorption of magnesium.

Another critical aspect to be careful about is that some elements react with one another, and form compounds that are difficult to absorb, which means that they have to be provided at different times.

With the above different variations, a hydroponic farmer must have a good grasp of the requirements of plants and the interaction of nutrients with each other, and with the plants themselves. They must carefully monitor the solutions they provide to the plants and check to see the changes in concentration that could come about. The alternative option is for the farmer to invest in an automated hydroponics system, which is quite expensive, to run the process on his or her behalf.

Farmers are also obliged to take great care of the solutions they are using to keep them from contamination by unwanted substances. Most choose to enclose the hydroponics project inside a greenhouse or a building to ensure that they alone have control of what is going on in the systems. This limitation also gives the farmers the liberty to optimize on the environmental influences of the plant, such as the light, carbon dioxide exposure and the temperatures, all to maximize the yields received.

This means that hydroponics is just not about growing crops without using soil; it also means that the farmer has absolute control of the plants and their growing process, at least.

Crops You Could Grow

If you are wondering what kind of crops you can grow using the hydroponic system, the simple answer is that you could grow any vegetable, fruit or houseplant you would want. The system, however, is best suited for crops that can grow well in hydroponic conditions.

The general rule is that the use of solution is best for plants that tend to have shallow roots. For example, you could grow some lettuce, radishes, herbs, or some spinach. The aggregate systems are best suited for crops that have a deep root system like beetroot, and those whose tops tend to be heavy like cucumbers, and squash. Other crops you could plant include tomatoes, strawberries, peppers, celery, and watercress.

Tomato varieties are particularly popular in this kind of farming because it is said that they bring forth larger fruits and that they grow indeterminately, which is to say that they will grow continually and repeatedly. You will always find fruit on their stems.

Farmers also tend to lean towards the disease-resistant crop varieties because the plants live longer and hence produce for a longer time.

Avoid growing plants that are not genetically suited to the hydroponic environment like wheat. Researchers found that for you to grow enough wheat to make a loaf of bread, you would need at least $23! That's too expensive.

The Growing Systems

Many innovative systems have been created to replace the traditional gravel bed that was taken up when people first started embracing hydroponics. When making a decision on which growing system you would wish to install, ensure that you take into account the economics of your agribusiness, space requirements of the plants, the type of crop that you would be growing, the support system and the growing time.

Once you have figured these details out, you can then decide on whether you wish to grow these plants in a greenhouse or growth room. Some farmers take both options and will use the growth room for germination purposes, after which the seedlings that come off the process are transferred to the greenhouse where they grow out as crops. The added advantage of this arrangement is that the heat emitted from the lights in the growth room redistributes into the greenhouse, heating and warming the air in there.

Some of the common growing material farmers use include:

Pipes and Troughs

Farmers use PVC pipes or open and closed plastic troughs to grow cucumbers, lettuce, and tomatoes. The troughs are either filled with just the nutrient solution, or they may be filled with vermiculite, perlite or peat moss. Some farmers mount these pipes or troughs on movable racks or rollers to enhance their spacing as they grow. In the case of PVC pipes, farmers prefer the 3-inch diameter kind that has 6-inch holes on the center to give enough room for the development of lettuce leaves. Majority of these troughs and pipes are 10 feet or 12 feet. The farmer then uses carts to move the pipes from the growing area to the packing room.

Stones or Sand Culture

This is the medium that is used for most of the plants that need a deep bed, that of about 18 to 23 inches. The bed is prepared by placing the pea stones, the trap rock, or the sand on a plastic-lined bed or trough that is sloping to one point to allow the excess nutrient solution to drain off. The minimum slope should be 2%. Once the farmer places the seedlings onto this medium, he then has to water with the nutrient solution several times during the day.

Beds

Hydroponics beds are plastic lined bed-like structures on whom the nutrient solution is pumped from one end, and flows to the other end. If you want to plant lettuce plants on beds like these, consider using foam polystyrene flats to help the plants float in the solution.

Trays

In this method, the trays are flooded with the nutrient solution periodically. The trays are suitable for growing crops that were started in 1 to 2-inch diameter growth blocks. Most farmers buy these plastic molded trays or those that are made from waterproof plywood.

Bags

Another option is to use polythene film bags, and filling them with a solution made with peat and vermiculite. The bags are then laid up in a trough, from one end to the other, and soaker hoses or drip tubes are inserted in them to deliver the nutrient solution. These bags can be reused several times before they are discarded.

Besides the plant support material mentioned above, there are other materials needed to complete various makes of the hydroponic systems used. Farmers will need controls, tanks, and pumps. The tanks should be made of inert material, such as plastic, concrete, or fiberglass because if the tanks were made of some reactive material, the reaction between the tank and the fertilizer solution would corrode the tank, pipes, and pumps.

The farmer can have manual switches and controls as simple as a time clock, or have a computer automated process where everything is adjusted automatically. The computer also adjusts the chemical content of the nutrient solution, in accordance with the nutrients that the plants are absorbing.

CHAPTER 2
Must Have Tools

As you venture into hydroponics farming, there are specific tools you need to get you started. Although there are several systems from which you shall choose, the kind of tools used in all of them is more or less the same.

The tools you will need include:

A Reservoir

From its name, the reservoir will be used for reserving the nutrient concentrate. The concentrate is typically a mixture of water and the required plant nutrients and depending on the kind of hydroponic system you choose to install; the liquid is pumped from it periodically into the growing chamber as set at the timers.

In some systems, the reservoir doubles as the growing chamber too, such that the plants grow suspending their roots in the nutrients concentrate 24 hours, every day.

You do not have to purchase a special reservoir; you can fashion it from almost any inert large container that you use to hold water, so long as it does not leak. The container should be able to hold enough of the solution to allow it to grow. In addition, the container should be opaque to prevent the rays of the sun from penetrating into the solution.

If the container available to you is not opaque, there are many ways to make it light proof. For example, you could wrap or cover it up with an opaque material, or you could paint over it. The idea behind the opaqueness is to prevent algae from growing on the inside of the container.

If the hustle of making your own reservoir seems a bit too much, you could also opt to purchase the commercial reservoirs, and they will serve you well.

A Growing Chamber

A growing chamber is one of the most critical parts of a hydroponic system because this is where the plant roots develop. The chamber is the container that holds the roots, provides support to the entire plant, and house the nutrient concentrate.

The chamber, just like the reservoir, should be kept from direct sunlight and extreme temperatures because these can introduce heat stress to the plants. In case of exposure to extreme temperatures, such as heat, the plants abort their fruits and flowers.

The size and shape of the growing chamber are dependent on the kind of hydroponic system you intend to run, and the plants you wish to grow. Plants that grow big roots will require a large growing chamber while those that develop small roots will be okay with just a small one. However, do not be stressed about sizes because any chamber size will make due so long as the plants you are growing get their deserved nutrients and space.

In your quest to find the best growing chamber, kindly keep off metallic containers because metals are subject to corrosion and they react with the nutrient concentrate. If you cannot purchase a commercial growing chamber, however, check around to see the non-metallic items you could transform into growing chambers. However, if you still need to maintain class and style while at it, you could opt for a commercial growing chamber; there are some fabulous makes available, and I am certain they will appeal to your pallet.

Delivery System

The delivery system is the system that delivers nutrients to the plant roots directly. The concept of this is quite simple, in fact, and can be customized to fit into any system you choose to take up and install. A typical delivery system must include connectors, PVC tubes, blue or black vinyl tubing, and tubing connectors, for garden irrigation.

Depending on the hydroponic system that you settle for, you can choose to use emitters and sprayers for the delivery system. Although the sprayers and emitters are quite useful, be prepared, however, for frequent clogs when the nutrients in the solution build up. Therefore, if you are looking forward to stress-free farming, avoid them as best as you can.

Submersible Pump

Most pumping systems have a submersible pump to regulate the pumping of the nutrient concentrate from the reservoir to the growing chamber. You can buy these pumps at home improvement stores or hydroponic shops in your area. The pumps come in varying sizes, and you just have to choose one that matches the size of your farm.

How do submersible pumps work, you ask? Well, the pumps are just impellers that take advantage of electromagnetic fields to spin then pump their water. It is easy to maintain them because the majority of the time, you are only required to clean the solution filter. If you bought your submersible pump without a filter, you could still make one by cutting some part of the furnace filter, ensuring that it fits the submersible pump.

Besides the filter, you also need to clean the pump occasionally to ensure that there are no clogs that would obstruct the nutrients as they flow to the plants.

Air Pump

Although it is not compulsory that you make an air pump part of your hydroponic system, you ought to give it a thought because it comes with so many benefits. An air pump is also widely available in stores, and inexpensive, particularly if you are able to buy yours at a store that sells aquarium supplies.

An air pump is primarily used to ensure that there is a steady supply of oxygen in the water so that the roots can absorb it for their respiration, in the growing chamber. The pump does this by pumping the air through the airlines, onto the air stones, which ten creates bubbles that bubble up into the nutrient solution.

In case you are using a water culture hydroponic system, for example, the air pump keeps the roots from drowning in the nutrient solution because they are kept suspended in it all day, every day. In other hydroponic systems, the air pumps are fitted into the reservoirs to keep pumping oxygen into the water, increasing the oxygen concentration in the water.

Since the air pumps pump all day, they cause constant movement, which keeps the water and nutrients in it in constant motion. The circulation that results from the process ensures that the nutrients dissolve into the water evenly, at all times. The presence of oxygen in the water is also good because it prevents the growth of pathogens and microbes.

Timer

Not all hydroponics farmers need to time their operations with a timer, based on their choice of hydroponics system and its location. If your system is to be situated indoors, for example, and you have installed artificial lighting, you need to install a timer that will turn the lights off or on.

Drip and aeroponics systems also need a timer to control their submersible pump that controls the process of draining and flooding. It is important to take note of the fact that some types of aeroponics would need some special kind of timer to work properly.

Although the light and standard pump timers work very well, it is better to opt for a timer that has a 15 amperes rating other than 10 amperes rating because the former is often heavy duty and will have a cover that effectively protects it from water. You only have to check at the back of the packaging of the timer you choose to ensure that you have made a good choice.

But for those who may have a battery backup, a digital timer is not preferred over an analog one because once you unplug it from the power source, it loses all the data previously stored in it. Analog timers are a better choice for the additional benefit of having on and off settings. Therefore, as you go out to purchase a timer, ensure that yours has pins all around the dial, so that you get the analog kind, and avoid future regrets.

Growing Medium

The growing medium is essentially the substance on which the plants grow. It provides physical support to the plants, just like soil does, only that it is inert, not containing any minerals or living organisms. Different systems demand different growing mediums. For example, while other systems use peat moss, Rockwool or lava stone as the growing medium, aeroponics system uses air as the growing medium.

Nevertheless, the right kind of medium is one that retains moisture in such a way that the water solution will not need to be pumped in continually, every single minute.

Growing Lights

Grow lights: you can have them you can stay without them. They are an optional part of the system because it all depends on where you intend to plant your garden. You may end up using natural light or having to take up artificial lighting for your plants. If possible, opt for natural lighting because it is free, and will not add to the cost of setup as you purchase the new equipment and its accompanying maintenance costs.

If, however, you cannot find any good lighting at the place you intend to plant your garden by having lots of exposure through the window or having a sunroom, or that the time of the year does not allow enough lighting through, you may need to include some supplemental artificial lighting in your set up budget.

Kindly realize that your ordinary bulbs cannot be used as grow lights: grow lights are specially made light bulbs that emit light containing special color spectrums that mimic natural light. Your plants will take in these color spectrums and use them to carry on the process of photosynthesis, hence the leaf growth, flower formation, and fruit growth. Realize also that the intensity and type of light that the plant has access to, by large, determines its photosynthetic abilities.

Most hydroponic kit systems will come with complimentary light fixtures, but if you are setting up a DIY (Do It Yourself) garden, piecing together the equipment you need, you will need to purchase lighting fixtures.

The most effective lighting for a hydroponics system is the High-Intensity Discharge (HID) light fixture made up of either Metal Halide (MH) bulbs or High-Pressure Sodium (HPS) bulbs. The HPS, in particular, emits a red or orange-looking light, which works well for plants, particularly in their vegetative growth stage.

Another type of lighting used is T5. It produces fluorescent light of a high output, and this lighting consumes low energy and only a little heat. The T5 is suitable for when growing plant cuttings, and for growing plants with short growth cycles.

Ensure that the light is kept on a time so that the lighting will go on and off at the same time, each day.

PH Testing Kit

If you don't test the pH of your nutrient solution from time to time, you will be running your farm purely by guesswork, subjecting your entire investment to a trial-and-error game. The reality is that for your plants to thrive in the hydroponic garden you have set up, there needs to be a balanced pH, and using a pH testing kit, you can regularly check on your garden to determine whether the pH of the nutrient solution is optimal. If the pH is too low, you can adjust by bringing it up, and if it's too high, you can lower it also.

On a related note, besides the pH meter, you will also need equipment to measure the temperature and the PPM of the water. You could also purchase the equipment you would need to measure the humidity and temperature of the grow room. If, for example, you find that you need to adjust the humidity in the room, use a dehumidifier or a humidifier, to ensure that the plants do not dry out and that they do not dampen.

A fan or any other equipment that can be used to improve the air circulation in the room would also be welcome. Although a small oscillating fan may work for a beginner, you will need a more sophisticated fan as your garden grows, one with an intake and an exhaust system.

The Nutrient Solution

While the nutrient solution is not a tool, you will need to set it aside as you set your tools aside, in readiness for the setup of your garden. As we have established many times so far, the nutrient solution will be the primary source of nutrients for your plants for them to thrive.

The nutrient solution provides three primary macronutrients that can be found in most fertilizers: potassium, phosphorus and nitrogen, and a host of 10 other micronutrients that may not be found in the fertilizers, yet the plants need them to survive, grow and reproduce. Some of these micronutrients include zinc, molybdenum, boron, copper, iron, chloride and manganese.

As a beginner, it may benefit you to purchase an already mixed solution offering a balance of all the nutrients mentioned above, but as you gain more experience, you will find it easier to mix create your own nutrient solution, one that will provide the plants with all the nutrients they require.

The fertilizers or nutrients used in the hydroponic system you can find in both dry and liquid forms, and there are both organic and synthetic kinds. Either type you choose will be dissolved in water to come up with the nutrient solution that we have associated with the hydroponic system severely.

As you look around the store, you will find that there are some specific fertilizers or nutrients specifically designed for hydroponic farming, and if you use them, you are bound to receive good results, provided you follow all instructions indicated on the packaging. Kindly avoid using standard soil fertilizers in a hydroponic system because their mixing formulas are specifically designed for garden soil, not for direct infusion into the roots as it happens in hydroponics.

While still on the point of hydroponic fertilizers, ensure that you choose the kind of hydroponic nutrient that is designed for your particular needs. For example, you will find that some fertilizers are designed for flowering plants, while others are good for promoting vegetative growth such as that used for lettuce. If you apply the latter to a flowering plant, you will promote the growth of the leaves rather than the formation, enlargement, and blossoming of flowers.

The Quality of the Water Used

The solubility of water and its ability to deliver the nutrients you dissolved into it is affected both by the salt level of the water, as can be seen from the PPM, and the water pH. Typically, hard water has a high mineral content, and this fact keeps it from dissolving the minerals as effectively as the water that has a low mineral content. Therefore, in the event that the water you have for your project is hard, you will need to filter it out to take out the high mineral content.

The ideal water pH for making the nutrient solution is between 5.8 and 6.2, which is somewhat acidic. If your water is not at this pH level, you can use some chemicals to adjust it so that the pH gets within this ideal range.

The Conditions of the Room

It is of utmost importance, and great value, that the hydroponic system be set in the right conditions. Some of the elements you ought to check to ensure that the conditions are right include the carbon dioxide levels, relative humidity, temperature, and air circulation.

The humidity level is ideal if it ranges between 40% to 60% relative humidity. If the humidity gets to higher levels, it may lead to the formation of powdery mildew and other kinds of fungi.

The ideal temperature should range from 68 to 70F. If the temperatures are higher, the plants will become stunted, and if it gets even higher, the roots may start to rot.

The level of carbon dioxide, CO_2, is of most importance in the grow room. The best way to ensure that there is an adequate supply of it is by ensuring that the room has a free flow of air. As your farm or garden becomes bigger, you could now begin to supplement the CO_2 levels in the room because the more the gas is available in the growth room, the faster the growth of crops.

A Greenhouse

Any serious hydroponics gardener should aim for the ultimate gardening tool, a greenhouse. A greenhouse offers a farmer lots of advantages including complete climatic control, a lot of growing room, and access to natural lighting. If you are serious about increasing the output from your hydroponics garden, then the greenhouse is the way to go. It may seem like an ambitious project at first, but the return is that you get to have a larger supply of nutritious, safe and high-quality food for your nutrition, and to supply to other people, in exchange for money.

Considerations to Make When Purchasing Hydroponic Tools and Equipment

Getting into the hydroponics world is a new exciting experience, and the results of your hard work can be very fulfilling, but only if you get into the trade the right way. If you make mistakes on your way in, hydroponics gardening may get quite challenging, intimidating and frustrating, especially if you get the wrong tools and equipment, the kind that does not match your needs. On the other side, you could end up purchasing equipment that is too expensive, so that it takes you very long to get a return on your investment.

Therefore, to avoid making mistakes, here are some important considerations you ought to make when deciding on the kind of tools and equipment you purchase:

1. The plants you intend to grow

It is likely that you already envision what would be in your farm once you set everything up. To ensure that your vision comes to life, your task now is to go ahead and look for hydroponics equipment that will help you bring your dream to life. You wouldn't want to buy shallow trays while you intend to plant plants that have large and thick roots. Likewise, you would not wish to spend your money in the purchase of some 8-inch deep buckets while you only intended to plant shallow-rooted plants.

For you to purchase the right kind of growing medium, fertilizer, and hydroponic system, the kind that would accommodate the plants you want to grow in terms of size and their growth rate, you need to consult a hydroponics expert. Many manufacturers of these things also give out some phone numbers from which you can contact hydroponic professionals about growing issues you may have.

2. The space available

Consider where you intend to be growing your crops. Do you want to set up a small greenhouse in your backyard, your basement, or do you intend to use some large closet? Prior to purchasing your equipment, ensure that you first calculate the size of the available space and determine just how much equipment can fit in the space you have determined. For example, if you intend to plant your crops in rows, ensure that the space available can allow at least a meter spacing between the plant rows to allow walking in between the rows as you tend to your garden.

3. Your budget

Before you walk into the shop and select the hydroponics equipment that best appeals to you, you need to take some time to determine the amount of money you can comfortably spend, and then try to make the best of that amount by creating a budget, and sticking to it. Keep in mind that the cost of buying tools and equipment is not the only cost you have to cover, factor in the cost of running the lights, the electricity bill, the labor costs, water bill, and the cost of replacing the equipment that could break down.

Sticking to a budget is not to mean that you should go cheap though because as you may have learned, cheap things are often the expensive ones. It will save you a lot of money in the long run if you choose to spend a little extra on the equipment when you purchase the best and highest quality ones on the market.

4. The time you have

Just like most people who engage in hydroponic farming as a hobby, you do not wish to spend your entire day at your garden. This is the reason you should consider just how well the hydroponics system you choose can function without your assistance before you purchase it. If you don't have time to wait it out or change systems manually, opt for a more mechanized automatic system that can run even when you are away.

Nevertheless, consider the risk of mechanizing the entire process. For example, if you chose the appealing aeroponics system, realize that if anything were to go wrong with your timer, there would be very quick drying out of the roots, which means that although the system can run by itself, it still requires as much attention as that in which everything is done manually.

Not everyone has the luxury of rushing home from work every now and then to check on their plants or to take countermeasures that could save the plants in the event there was a power outage. Therefore, if this is your life, opt for a system that gives you a large margin of error such as one whose medium can hold air and water very well.

Overall, besides the tools and equipment you need, the primary things to have include the hydroponic water concentrate where all the nutrients your plants would need are. In case you have chosen a system that recycles the nutrient solution, ensure that you change it at the end of every week or two, at most, so that the nutrients remain balanced.

If you are to grow your plants indoors, you will need supplemental lighting most of the time, and for a garden growing green vegetables, it would be nice if you installed a fluorescent cool-white shop light just a few inches above the plants for it to work very well. If you are planting crops that produce fruits and flowers, you also must provide a grow light or else they won't grow to maturity.

CHAPTER 3
Types Of Hydroponic Systems

One of the primary advantages of hydroponic farming is its versatility meaning that there is a large number of systems from which a farmer can choose from. The decision of which hydroponic system to choose is based on your needs, the plants you wish to grow, your budget, and the space you have set aside for the project.

Aeroponics

The aeroponics hydroponics system is the most high-tech of the possible setups, but this is not to mean that they are complex: once you understand how the system works, the rest is easy. In this method, the plants' roots hang loose in the air and are occasionally sprayed with the nutrient concentrate. There are two ways to do it: using a pond flogger and using a spray nozzle, to spray onto the roots. If you opt for a pond flogger, ensure that the flogger has been coated using Teflon because the coating makes it easier to maintain.

Some farmers time the misting cycles just like the ebb and flow hydroponics system, only that the aeroponics cycle is much shorter because the mistings are only minutes apart. If you have a very fine sprayer, however, it is possible to mist the roots continuously so that an even larger amount of oxygen is available to the roots.

The use of the aeroponics systems has shown that plants grow even quicker using this method in comparison to the simpler systems like the deep-water culture, although this is yet to be verified across the spectrum. In case you want to try this method out for yourself, ensure that you purchase finer sprayer nozzles than the typical ones, to help you atomize the solution.

The Advantages of Aeroponics

- Exposing the roots increases their access to oxygen, which is unlike other methods that submerge the plants' root systems in the nutrient solution

- This method saves on nutrients, water, and the growing medium

- It is cost effective and efficient, especially when you finish carrying out the initial setup

Disadvantages of Aeroponics

- At the very slightest interruption, suppose the high-pressure nozzles failed, the roots can dry out, and the effect can be even more severe than what would happen if you had the N.F.T. system setup.

- The timers and the pump need regular inspection, which causes the system to be quite demanding in terms of maintenance.

- The aeroponics system is not as easy or cheap to set up as other methods are.

What You Would Need to Start an Aeroponics System as A DIY

- A solution reservoir
- PH kit
- Mist nozzles, sprinklers or sprayers
- A fitted lid to keep the moisture in submersible pump that has tubing whose ends have mist sprayers.
- A timer that will activate the sprayers at regular intervals
- A nutrient kit

Nutrient Film Technique (N.F.T.)

In these systems, the farmer grows his or her crops in tubes called gullies. Alternatively, the farmer can also use grow tanks to increase the speed at which the roots are growing. The gully, or the growing tray, must be placed above the reservoir, at an angle, and ideally, a channel is created at the center of the grow tray so that it can be used to drain the solution with more efficiency.

The nutrient solution is pumped into the growing channels and it runs along the bottom of the channel. However, when the solution gets to the end of the channel, it falls back into the main reservoir and the pump sends the solution back again to the beginning of the system. This movement creates a recirculating system, like the one used in deep water culture.

This system does not need a timer because the pump effectively ensures a constant supply of nutrients to the plant roots. The plants only need to be situated in their net pots, and they do not require a growing medium; they are suspended in the air too, just as in the aeroponics setup. However, in the N.F.T system, the plants can only be harvested or replaced one after the other.

The nutrient solution must be kept aerated by use of an air pump and an air stone. The constant bubbling also helps to prevent the solution from settling while providing the roots with the oxygen they need to aid in the process of nutrient absorption, so that the plant will use less energy in sourcing for the nutrients it needs, and more energy in growing and producing fruit.

Having a submersible pump at the reservoir also helps to ensure that the nutrient solution is constantly supplied to the grow tray. Having a gap between the water and the plants also guarantees aeration before the water drains off back into the reservoir. The NFT is certainly an improvement of the drip system, as you shall see next.

Benefit of the N.F.T

- This technique is cost effective because it does not require a growing medium, and because the nutrient solution that is used is often recycled and recovered back to the reservoir.

Disadvantages of the N.F.T

- The cost of maintenance, in this case, is higher because the pumps need regular supervision to ensure that they are working well as it should be.

- In the event that there is an interruption of the power supply, the roots will dry out very quickly, particularly because the method does not use any growing medium.

- Some roots tend to overgrow and they clog the channels.

What You Would Need to Set Up an N.F.T System

- A nutrient kit
- A reservoir
- A pH kit
- Gullies or grow tanks, from which you grow the plants
- Tubes to direct the nutrient solution from the channel and into the reservoir tank
- Tubing and pump to direct the nutrient solution from the reservoir to the plants
- A spreader mat (this one is optional), to boost nutrient absorption
- A platform or a table to hold the gullies, together with a channel, that can be used to direct the nutrients back into the reservoir.

The Ebb and Flow Hydroponics System

The Ebb and Flow system, sometimes called the Flood and Drain system is more advanced and more complicated than any other. In it, the plants are placed in a grow tray in the growing medium and then placed at the top of the reservoir. There is also a scheduled timer, which causes the pump to switch on and flood the grow tray with the nutrient solution drawn from the reservoir, in regular intervals. Once the grow tray floods, the timer switches off, and the nutrient solution drains off.

The Ebb and Flow hydroponics system are either set as a recovery or as a non-recovery system to mean that the solution could be used only once and discarded, or that it could be collected and reused.

The frequency of flooding for this method depends on factors like the amount of water that the plants need, the size of the plants, where your plants stand in the growth cycle, and the temperature in the air.

The flooding cycle is easy. It starts with having a water pump, the reservoir placed underneath the grow tray and a timer to determine the frequency of flooding. Once you flood the tray, the law of gravity will order the excess solution back to the reservoir below, where it will be oxygenated by both the air stone and the air pump. The solution then sits in the reservoir, in readiness for the next flooding cycle.

Hydroponic farmers who choose the ebb and flow system do so for the flexibility of the system. The system allows the tray to fill with the growing medium of choice, and for the farmers to organize their plants in net pots. They also get better control of the plants' roots.

Advantages of the Ebb and Flow Hydroponics System

- The system allows the efficient use of energy and water
- It can be customized to match your needs
- It is easy to control the temperature of the project because it is set up indoors and because the reservoir is differently placed from the growing trays.

- The plants enjoy good aeration because they are not fully submerged in the nutrient solution, while at the same time, they get to enjoy absorption of nutrients at regular times.

- Since the plants do not have a direct connection to the reservoir, it is possible to grow a larger proportion of crops than the reservoir can hold.

Disadvantages of the Ebb and Flow Hydroponics System

- The system uses a great deal of the growing medium

- In case of a power supply disruption, the pumps and the timers will be affected, causing the roots to dry up. However, this problem can be resolved by simply choosing mediums that ideally take in and retain moisture in an efficient way.

- A farmer needs to have some level of experience maintaining the pH and nutrient levels and to ensure that the system, including the medium, does not clog with the salts contained in the nutrient solution.

Drip Irrigation System

The drip irrigation system is one of the more popular hydroponic systems. The system is set up to enable the transportation of nutrients from the reservoir using a tube down to an irrigation pipe that waters the plant's base.

Drip irrigation may recover the nutrient solution, or not. Home growers tend to lean towards recovery while commercial growers lean towards non-recovery.

Advantages of the Drip System

- A relatively cheap method
- The farmer has greater control of the watering and feeding schedule

- Less likely to break down
- It is possible to set the timers so precisely that the plants will be let until when more of the solution is needed

Disadvantages of the Drip System

- For a small garden, a drip system is slightly overkill
- The nutrients and pH levels tend to fluctuate, especially when using a recirculating system
- There is a high level of waste, especially if using a non-recovery method
- If the farmer takes the non-recovery option, the cost of purchasing nutrients may get so high

What You Need to Set Up the Drip Irrigation System

- A timer
- PH kit
- Growing medium
- Containers or growing trays for the plants
- Reservoir container to house the nutrient solution
- Air pump that contains air stones and tubing
- Drip lines and irrigation pipes with sets of joiners and adapters
- Nutrient kit
- Submersible pump and tubing to deliver the nutrients

The Wick System

The wick system is a naturally passive system. There are no moving parts that require automation, and hence no electricity is required to run activities and functions. This makes the wick system a perfect selection for persons that are just getting their feet wet, and those working with a tight budget.

The wick system is the simplest of them all. It works by causing the plant to receive nutrients using a wick that is attached to the reservoir on one end, and the plant on the other end. When the end in the reservoir soaks up, it transports the nutrient solution through the fiber of the wick, on to the plant.

One trick for succeeding in the use of a wick system is to use a growing media that is able to transport nutrients and water well. Some of the excellent options from which you may choose from include perlite, coconut coir, and vermiculite.

Advantages of the Wick System

- Easy to set up
- Excellent pick for beginners and children
- Affordable
- Once you have set it up correctly, this is a truly hands-off method
- The wick system is especially suited for small plants, those with lesser nutritional needs

Disadvantages of the Wick System

- Is not suited to larger plants that have higher nutrient requirements because they may need much more moisture and nutrient than the wick is able to deliver

- The wick system does not make the process of controlling the humidity of the growing room easy

- The system may cause uneven absorption of nutrients, and with time, there could be a buildup of nutrients in the growing medium

- If the wick is improperly placed, it could mean death for your crops

What You Would Need to Set Up a Wick System

- A nutrient kit
- A bucket, reservoir, or just a tub with a lid

- Some growing medium
- Basket or container
- A wick could be a rope, or any other absorbent material

The Deep-Water Culture System

Of all the active systems we have discussed, the deep-water culture system is the simplest of them all. It is a system in which many plants are placed on a tray, ideally made of polystyrene, which then floats at the top of the nutrient solution that has been held in a solution reservoir. In this setup, the plant's roots will be completely submerged in the water.

Instead of the polystyrene sheet, the plants can also be placed in net pots and the pots can be fitted into a lid that will fit the circumference of the reservoir, tank or tub in use.

An air stone connected to an air pump is used to keep the nutrient solution below oxygenated, which ensures that the plants' roots do not become waterlogged to the point that they would rot and be incapable of absorbing the nutrients below.

Plants that are best suited for this setup include Asian greens, lettuce, endives, and rocket, among others.

Advantages of the Deep-Water Culture System

- Affordable
- Easy to build
- Management is easy
- Requires only a small space
- Suited for beginners
- Suitable for commercial hydroponics farming
- Ideal for plants with short growing periods
- Less wastage because the system reuses the same nutrient solution

Disadvantages of Deep-Water Culture System

- Not suited for large plants
- Not suited to plants that have long growing periods

What You Need to Set Up the Deep-Water Culture System

- Air pump
- System-specific reservoirs
- PH kit
- Nutrient kit
- Air stone
- Air pump
- Growing medium

The above systems are the six major hydroponics systems types. You can clearly read how each works, and the advantages and disadvantages of each system.

Do not be anxious about which method you choose though because no matter the method you choose, provided you provide proper care. Your plants will grow very big, and very fast. With any of these systems, you will assuredly experience the ups that hydroponics offer, particularly the flexibility, so that whenever you are having trouble, you will have no reservations about correcting them and getting your farm back on the right track.

Advanced Hydroponic Systems

The above six hydroponics systems are best suited for beginners, and for your knowledge, we will discuss three more hydroponic systems in brief, so that you do not confuse between the beginners' and advanced kind.

The systems include:

The Kratky Method

The Kratky method is one that combines the deep-water culture system and the wick system. It brings in the constant adequate supply advantage of the deep-water culture system added to the passivity and low maintenance of the wick system.

In the Kratky method, the plants are held in a net pot, on top of anon-circulating solution reservoir that has a tight-fitting lid. The net pot is fitted into a hole that has been cut out of the lid. At first, the roots are submerged beneath the solution, and only a small air gap is left between the nutrient solution and the inside of the lid.

Once this is done, the farmer then leaves the system alone, and as the plant and the growing medium absorb the right nutrients, the roots of the plant grow, the water level falls and the space between the solution and the inside of the lid gets bigger. This space ensures that the plant receives the nutrition it needs from the solution while getting enough oxygen supply.

Advantages

- This method can be a good way for beginners to get into hydroponics farming
- It almost requires zero maintenance
- The method is affordable

Disadvantages

- Only suited for small foliage crops
- Not ideal for large scale farming

Fogponics

Fogponics is a great improvement of aeroponics, evidenced by the improved farming results. Fogponics has improved farming rapidly.

It works this way: rather than creating a mist at specified intervals, the farmer installs a fogger in the reservoir to create a humidified environment. The fogger, or the mist maker, as you can tell, changes the size of water droplets to the point that they become a mist or fog, which is then directed to the plants' root system.

The new gravity-defying nutrient solution droplets offer the plant a full nutrient coverage to the point that it stimulates the development of new root hairs as an adaptation, to increase the surface area of the root system, for greater absorption of the nutrients.

Advantages of the Fogponics System

- Reduces the water and nutrients usage by more than 40 percent
- Economical
- Easy to set up
- The nutrient solution does not reduce in concentration because the recirculation is not used up.

Disadvantages of Fogponics

- The cost of the initial setup is quite high
- The mist is very light, yet it must be contained
- In case there is a power outage, the havoc wreaked to the crops can be ridiculously big
- The setup requires regular cleaning of the equipment, and this increases the cost of maintenance

The Dutch Bucket System

The Dutch Bucket System is an adaptation of the Ebb and Flow system, only that it uses individual buckets placed in rows, and one irrigation line supplying nutrients from above, while a drainage pipe is located below the pipe, directing the liquid that drains back to the solution reservoir.

The Dutch Bucket System is suited for large operations because the individual rows can be joined to form one irrigation line that can easily accommodate large plants that bear fruit. Each plant is given its own bucket, and this makes it easy to move individual plants around. If you choose this system, you will want to have a growing medium that is capable of maintaining high moisture levels as well as be well aerated. Ensuring that the drainage is doing well is also essential because it prevents clogging so that the nutrients that are not absorbed into the plant can easily drain back into the nutrient solution reservoir.

The process of getting the excess solution back to the reservoir depends on gravity, but the process of getting the solution from the reservoir up onto the plant relies on a submersible pump placed at the bottom of the reservoir. An air pump and an air stone are also required to keep the solution in the reservoir oxygenated. In addition, salt and pH levels should be checked occasionally and maintained at a balance.

When it comes to choosing the ideal growing medium, you have a number of options. The seedlings, you can start off, using sphagnum peat, Rockwool or coco peat, and a water culture system. Once the seedlings have grown a bit and established themselves, you can then transfer them to a propagation area of the Dutch Bucket System.

You could also choose perlite. It is light, has excellent water and air retention, and drains excess fluid well. However, the farmer still needs to put measures in place to prevent blockage. It might help to cover the entrance of the drainage pipe with mesh. However, it is important to note that perlite works best when mixed with a medium like vermiculite

Another ideal medium for the Dutch Bucket System is Light Expanded Clay Aggregate (LECA). This medium is ideal due to its large pebbles because they cannot get stuck in the drain pipe, causing blockage of the circulation system.

In your search for a good growing medium, avoid coconut coir because it is highly absorbent, and its drainage is slow. The coir is suitable for a drain to waste system and not one that relies on flooding. If you wanted to use it, you would have to convert your system into a low volume or slow drip hydroponic system, and this would increase the running costs and beat the purpose of having a recovery system because the nutrient solution would not be recycled.

Advantages of the Dutch Bucket System

- Saves on water
- It is best if you are going large scale on your farming
- It boosts plant growth

Disadvantages of the Dutch Bucket System

- The cost of maintenance is high
- Expensive, because it requires high-quality machinery to succeed

CHAPTER 4
Advantages and Disadvantages of Hydroponics

Regardless of your crop production scale, hydroponics is for you. It would make an excellent choice for you because it accords you the freedom to vary and control the factors that determine the growth rate of your crops. Any day, any time, a fine-tuned hydroponic system will outdo soil-based agriculture in terms of the quality, quantity, yield, and the amount of space that the plants need to have to be productive.

Without politicking or appealing to your sentiments, take it that if you feel the need to grow some of the biggest, juiciest and the yummiest produce, you have to try hydroponics.

The process of getting the system on the ground might appear challenging at first, but the results you get make it all worth it. It is worth the time, money, and effort. The only thing you have to do is start small, and gradually watch as your dream comes to life.

Here are some of the Benefits you should expect to enjoy:

The Yields Are Higher

One of the most prominent benefits of hydroponics is the increased productivity of your farm and your crops. In a well-placed hydroponic system, expect the produce to be at least 30% higher than that of plants grown directly from the soil.

Plants Grow Quicker

What would happen if a child got the proper nutrition, did not fall ill and got enough rest? What would be the case if a business was situated in a place with a high demand for its products, the customer service was excellent, and the people could afford what is being sold? The result in the two scenarios is that growth would be quite high.

The plants are able to grow faster and bigger because they do not have to work harder to get the nutrients they need for growth. Even a small root system will be sufficient for delivering the required nutrients to the plants, so the plants do not have to advance their root systems to reach nutrients far below on the soil. Therefore, the only task the plant has is to develop upwards and produce its fruits. It is said that hydroponic plants grow at least 25% faster than those grown the traditional way.

Does Not Require a Yard

When people think about farming, the first thing that comes to mind are large tracts of land, or a yard, at the very least. However, even people without yards can grow their crops. Hydroponics allows you to plant your crops indoors. For example, you could transform the extra space you have in your house to a veggie or flower garden.

Saves Water

Since the hydroponics system, you will build is not exposed to weather elements, there is less water evaporation. This means that plants get to utilize less water than if you had planted them on the soil, outside. This makes hydroponics an environmentally friendly method for growing crops.

Production Can Be Done All-Year-Round

Using a hydroponics system puts the seasons in your hands, under your control. You do not have limitations in regards to when you can sow or harvest your produce because you will be using an internally controlled setup. However hard the winter hits or the summer burns itself, you are guaranteed that you will get what you have been working towards.

The ability to produce all-year-round allows the commercial farmer to eliminate risks involved in the business such as the effects of a poor crop season, and also ensures continuous production and accessibility of food to the farmers and others in the community.

Requires Less Labor

While hydroponics farming is capital intensive, less labor is needed. For example, you will not need to hire labor to weed your plants because this function is already automated.

In addition to reduced labor, hydroponics makes it easy to provide the little labor needed. This is because the systems can be constructed or placed on heights that are simpler to access. The farmer is not limited to growing his crops from the ground, because the plants can be placed on heights that are comfortable relative to the farmer's body. This way, the labor of weeding, planting or transporting becomes much easier.

Does Not Require Any Soil

This is a distinct advantage particularly in areas where the existing field soil is poor. It is also an advantage for people living in apartments because growing plants with soil can be quite inconveniencing.

The absence of soil also means that the plants and the produce are cleaner.

Requires Less Space

When using this system of agriculture, your plants will not develop an extensive root system that they would typically need to reach nutrients down below. Since plants are spaced out to give enough room to each plant's rooting system, the hydroponics plants can be planted close together. This is another advantage, in favor of indoor planting.

You also have the opportunity to move the plants as they grow, and this will guarantee an increase in the density of the crops. For example, let's say you are using growth room for germination and the production of seedlings. Now, if the density of some particular crops in the greenhouse decreases, the average area a plant will need in comparison to conventional crop production.

Less Wastage

Hydroponic crops are known to absorb all the mineral nutrients that are provided in the solution used, without any wastage, and hence this kind of farming produces less pollution.

Produces Higher Quality Yields

The produce collected from hydroponics is of higher quality in comparison to conventional farming because the plants have access to all the resources they would need to produce at maximum capacity.

When combined with greenhouse, it produces even better results. Hydroponics is all about control, and a greenhouse provides an excellent environment to allow it.

Hydroponics Farming Is Eco-Friendly

Water used in a hydroponic system can always be recycled, and because of this, a hydroponic system takes up only about 10% of the water that normal conventionally grown crops take up.

Another advantage is that since this is a closed system, nutrients applied do not leach away, which causes the hydroponics to use up only 25% of the fertilizers that regular farms apply

Farmers Do Not Have to Deal with Eutrophication When They Take Up Hydroponics

Eutrophication is the dense growth of aquatic plants such as algae that grow due to the run-off of fertilizers

Farmers Do Not Have to Deal with Soil Pests and Diseases

Even if there are natural predators, the use of a greenhouse makes it easier to control the pests. In the same way, a building with four walls and a roof creates a barrier that keeps off pests. Hence, there are artificial pesticides required. This is also the case for plant diseases.

Without soil acting as a medium, the likelihood of spreading and contracting diseases reduces significantly. As such, there is no need to fumigate the crops or to weed. There will also not be any microorganisms because there is not a soil stratum.

The failure to use herbicides and pesticides allows the farmer to grow cleaner food, promoting the health of the food consumers.

Hydroponics Makes Agriculture Feasible in Areas That Are Not Naturally Suited to Farming

The high-water efficiency of the hydroponics system makes it possible and easy to farm in arid environments. The farmer only has to stock the hydroponic trays on top of each other, and place the plants closer to each other, side by side, making the growing trays, and the entire system more space-efficient than regular farming.

Since it is possible to control, artificially, almost all environmental conditions, people who wish to get into farming can take up almost all kinds of spaces available such as disused railway tunnels, uninhabited buildings, and other unusual spaces.

In addition, now that commercial hydroponic farmers do not have any limitations, and plant their crops on rural agricultural land, food growers can now plant their crops closer to their markets, and the increased accessibility takes out the need for complex distribution that reduces the farmer's profit margin, and introduces third parties, the brokers.

Hydroponics Reduce the Need to Transport Food Items

Since anyone can become a farmer and can grow crops even far from their habitats, at a place that is in proximity to the consumers, the need for transportation is reduced, and so are the fuel emissions, hence allowing the people to enjoy both fresh produce and clean air.

Monoculture Is Allowed

Typically, growing the same crops all the time will exhaust the soil of particular elements, which either changes the soil pH or reduces the yields because the plants cannot access the nutrients they need. However, in hydroponics, farmers need not worry that they could exhaust the soil of a particular element when they plant one type of crop recurrently. Farmers need not rotate their crops, and they can instead focus wholly on the production of food items in demand, those that will fetch them some good money.

The quick succession of crops is also attributed to the fact that the system does not require a restoration period as land does. Therefore, immediately a farmer pulls out one plant, he can quickly plant another in its stead. This ensures that the farmer will have the maximum possible yields per square foot.

There Are No Weeds

One of the most back-breaking tasks associated with farming is the process of combating weeds. It consumes the farmer's time. When using hydroponics, the likelihood that your farm will grow weeds is quite low because the weeds seeds that are often found in the soil are not there. This is also an advantage to your crop because it grows unopposed, not having to fight for resources. Hence, it grows fast and produces higher than normal yields.

It Is Easy to Maintain Hydroponic Systems

Resources are used efficiently and effectively when using a hydroponics system. The water used to water the plants is recycled and the fertilizers used are the actual amounts, hence no wastage. It is easy to measure fertilizer and to determine the proportions of its constituent elements, which means that the farmer doesn't work out of guesswork. You will know when your plants have the right fertilizer concentration, and when there isn't a correct measure, you only have to adjust the amount that you have applied.

Easier to Control the Costs of Farming

Since only little, if any, nutrients are lost, the farmer only has to use a little of the fertilizer, among other resources. In addition, the plants have faster growth, which leads to higher yields.

Ph Control

Since the nutrients are administered through a water solution, it is easier to measure, monitor and adjust your solution's pH levels in comparison to when applying fertilizer to the soil directly in rural farming.

Hydroponics Is Fun and Makes for an Interesting Hobby

Dealing in hydroponics or any other nature activity puts you back in sync with nature. If you are tired from your daily activities, it is relieving to go back home and observe how your garden is progressing: weeding, watering the plants and harvesting the produce. Activities like these are great stress-relievers and can surely turn your day around. You could also set your pot on the stove and start preparing the tastiest and freshest vegetables and herbs or enjoy a bowl of fruit from your green space.

Disadvantages of Hydroponics

Requires Technical Knowledge and Experience

When running a hydroponics system, realize that you are running a system composed of many kinds of equipment, and this requires you to have specific expertise and knowledge of the devices you are to use, the plants you are to grow, and the mechanism of how these plants are to grow in the soilless environment. If you make mistakes in regard to setting up the systems or how you plan out your care of the crops, you may end up losing out on your investment.

There Are Risks Related to Electricity and Water

A hydroponics system primarily depends on water and electricity to operate. The combination of water and electricity, however, is a recipe for disaster, especially because they are used in such close proximity. Therefore, whenever you are working with electricity and the water systems equipment together, consider safety measures first.

The Initial Expenses Are Quite High

As you start out your hydroponics farm, you are sure to spend some considerable amount (the scale of your farming will also matter), to set up the space to be used for farming and to purchase the equipment needed. Whichever hydroponics system you take up, you will also need a pump, growing media, fertilizers, containers, lights, and seeds or seedlings.

Once your system is in place, you will only be paying for electricity, water, nutrients, and seedlings, as needed.

The Costs of Running Are Also Quite High

The control systems of the hydroponic garden, which would include the water purifiers, pumps, heaters, lights, and others, are electronically powered, and this costs money. In traditional farming, the water, the heat, and the light are naturally provided, and they are free, which makes them an added cost.

It Takes a While for You to Get a Return on Your Investment

Just recently, large scale hydroponic farms have been coming up, which shows that people now believe in the productivity of the soilless farms. That's a great development for agriculture and the development of hydroponics also. However, the issue is that the commercial growers setting up large-scale hydroponic farms will have to wait longer to receive a return on their investment.

The cost of setting up the large farms is particularly high, and the returns can be uncertain at times. As such, it would be difficult to come up with a profitable clear plan that would justify the investment while there are other attractive investment opportunities out there that would give a return on investment quicker, and more certainly than hydroponics farming.

Diseases and Pests Spread Quickly

Since you will be growing plants in a closed damp place, in the event that pests and infections come along, they can spread and escalate very fast among plants that are in the same nutrient reservoir.

In a small system, the pests or diseases would not cause so much havoc, which means that it is not quite a problem for beginners because you are advised to start small. For big farms, the issue could become problematic since the water is filtered and then recycled throughout the farm. Therefore, if a diseased plant is present in one section of the farm, it will infect the remaining area and could kill the entire crop in hours. Many large-scale farmers have lost their entire crop this way, which has made disease-control one of the critical factors to look out for when investing in hydroponics. All farmers, particularly those operating on a large scale, ought to have a proper disease and pest management plan early enough.

One of the best preventative measures is to ensure cleanliness in the farm. For one, only use clean pathogen-free water and growing materials, clean and check the hydroponic systems periodically. In case the diseases occur, you need to sterilize the infected nutrients, water, and the entire hydroponic system.

The downside of this cleanliness and sterilization exercise is that the water might also contain good microorganisms, and unfortunately, when the water is sterilized, it is impossible to eliminate the harmful streaks of bacteria and fungi and leave out the good ones; they all go out in the same swipe. In addition, the sterility of the water and the entire farm at large is only as good as the sterilization method that the farmer uses; the water could retain some harmful microorganisms.

Threats of System Failure

Farmers use electricity to manage the entire system and should take precautionary measures to prepare for a possible power outage. This is because were there to be a power outage or electrical failure, the entire system would stop working immediately, and the plants would dry out quickly, and die in a matter of hours. Therefore, farmers ought to have ready plans to prepare for power-related issues by having a backup power source, particularly those operating under large-scale systems. Most farmers opt to have several long-standing back-up generators that can run for a long time in case of an electrical emergency.

The Organic Question

There have been debates on whether crops grown under hydroponic systems can be labeled as organic or not. Some people raised questions as to whether plants grown as hydroponics get microbiomes as those that are grown in the soil.

Whatever the case, the fact remains that people have grown hydroponic crops all over the world including tomatoes, lettuce, strawberries, and others, for many years, and distributing them to the Netherlands, the United States, Australia, Tokyo, and other regions. This product has fed millions of people, and it poses fewer risks in regard to pesticides, pests, and diseases, compared to soil-grown crops.

Some suggestions into how hydroponics growers can turn their agriculture into an organic venture have been laid out, and some farmers have taken up this idea. Some have gone ahead to introduce microbiomes to the soil in the form of organic growing media such as coco coir, then adding worm casting into it. Others introduce natural nutrients instead of fertilizer in the form of alfalfas, neems, cotton seeds, fishes, and bones.

As for the organic debate though, there is yet to be a consensus on what qualifies to be organic and what does not, and as research continues to be carried out, we can hope to have a conclusive answer in the near future.

Requires a Heavy Investment of Time and Commitment

Just like any other worthwhile thing in life that requires hard work and a positive attitude to obtain any success, hydroponics requires your utmost dedication to attain the success that you anticipated. Plants that are planted on soil do not demand as much attention and dedication and can be left alone for many days and weeks, and they will continue to grow. The soil, together with Mother Nature, balance out whatever needs balancing.

The case of hydroponics is different. If the plants do not receive all the care and attention they need, they begin to die out. The plants are purely dependent on the farmer for survival, which means that the farmer must be equipped with the proper knowledge and expertise to care for them. Initially, farmers are advised to care for the plants themselves, and they can automate at a later time, once the system is up and running.

Hydroponics Limit Agricultural Production

Although growing your crops all year round increases the yield significantly, the space available remains an impediment to the amount you could possibly produce. In addition, the fact that you can plant more crops in a single space does not mean that the crops can be overcrowded; the plant still needs some space to enable it spread out, which means that there is still a limited number of crops you can plant at a time.

The Entire Hydroponic System Is Quite Vulnerable

As mentioned earlier, it only takes a few hours without power and the plants begin to dry out and die. In a system where the plants are exposed, if the plants are left unwatered for some hours, the drying out will be especially quick.

In addition, it is more likely to have pH and nutrient imbalances when using a solution as their source in comparison to when you use soil. If these imbalances happen, an entire crop could be wiped out very fast, and so is the situation in case of water contamination by either microorganisms or disease.

Requires Some Knowledge and Expertise

A farmer who wishes to venture into hydroponic farming needs to understand the entire process and the techniques used, and this can be quite complicated to grasp.

As you have seen, hydroponics farming stands to give you a number of advantages, but will still subject you to some disadvantages. If you still feel the need to press on and start your farm, go ahead and get started, there will always be a way around the challenges you face. Nothing should keep you from enjoying and selling to others the juicier, larger, tastier, and more nutritious foods you have been dying to try growing using the hydroponics method.

You also should ensure that you contact the local agricultural department to determine the requirements set for farm operations, as well as be informed of any existing risk of encountering fungi, bacteria, and other common diseases. Keep in mind that the most important lessons are learned by trial and error so that as you encounter challenges, you will keep learning and pushing yourself forward. In the end, your dream of successfully running a piece of this revolutionary method of agriculture will come to be.

CHAPTER 5
Getting Your Feet Wet

You know what hydroponic farming is, the tools you would need, and the systems from which you would choose, and this has aroused your interest in hydroponics farming, or that your heart did not sink, and you are still interested in following it through. Now, here is some more information to help you make your move into the business more graceful because it is by making the rights steps that you would succeed.

The right steps are:

1. Select The Right Seeds And Plants For Your Venture

You think that the hydroponics business is lucrative or you would want to venture into it to grow crops for you and your family's nutrition. However, what crops are you looking to grow? The answer you give to this question will determine what you do from now on, starting with the amount of money you set aside for the construction, the hydroponic system you choose, the amount of space you set aside, and the lighting. Different hydroponic systems work better than others for specific plant kinds.

For beginners, I recommend that they first try growing leafy veggies such as lettuce. Begin germinating your seeds in rapid rooter cubes because these cubes and once the seedlings are up, and after growing for several weeks, once you are sure that your plant has a healthy root system, now transfer the plants into your growth tray.

2. Choose The Appropriate Hydroponic System For Your Garden

You need to choose the hydroponic system early enough so that you may get some time to learn more about the setup and how it works. Read the alternatives too, and compare one to another, until you are able to choose the most appropriate of them.

The set up you pick will be determined by a few factors. The kind of plants you intend to grow, the amount of space that you have available, the number of plants you want to grow, and the budget you have. Even when your resources can allow you to start big, it is better to start small and then expand your craft in the future. As you start your garden, you will realize that there are many other new things to learn, and you might make some mistakes. It would be incredibly hurtful if anything bad happened while you had too many plants.

3. Choose the Light Source You Will Be Using

Lighting is a major factor and determinant of the success of your hydroponic garden. If you are not using natural light from the sun as your source of light, then you need to choose a hydroponic light from the market. There are some considerations to make though, because there are many kinds of lights in the market, and each has its unique advantages and disadvantages.

Kindly engage in some research to determine the light setup that will work best for the plants you intend to grow. Even then, you need to make some useful considerations such as light intensity, cost, coverage area, and the light spectrum. If you want fast growth and for the produce to be of high quality, it is best not to take the cheapest route in choosing the appropriate lighting.

If you cannot choose a light yourself, possibly from not knowing where to start, I suggest you get a full spectrum LED grow light. The light is cheap and suitable for leafy green plants and plants that produce fruit, and the lights are quite efficient. Don't forget to buy a timer, to go along with it too.

4. Choose The Hydroponic Medium

Once you have settled on your hydroponic setup, you now have to choose the growing medium you prefer, selecting from the options that would best work with the system you have chosen. The kinds that you should lean towards are those that are suitable for the plants you intend to be growing and the kind of system you have on.

There are different kinds of growing mediums, each with its own advantages. However, some of the factors to consider about the growing medium you choose include its water retention, pH stability, cost, and level of aeration. If you have problems choosing, then kindly take up hydroton expanded clay pebble because of their versatility. They work well with different kinds of hydroponic setups and different kinds of plants.

5. Purchase The Hydroponic Nutrients And Additives You Will Use In Your Garden

There are many nutrient concentrations and combinations, coming in 1, 2, and 3 part systems, and you make your choice based on the research you have conducted on what the plants would need. For beginners, you would be safe sticking with a 1-part nutrient solution, but if you feel that you have a good understanding of the nutrients the plants need, go ahead and take up even a 3 part nutrient solution. Most companies will have attached a feeding schedule on the product or their company websites, and you can follow up from there.

Additives are also very important because they assist in the process of sterilization of the system. They also affect your plants' growth rate, taste, and the size to which your plant grows. Think of additives as your plants' vitamins, and although they are not a critical part of your agriculture, they provide an extra boost to them.

6. Get A PH Meter And A PH Up/Down

As we have discussed prior, plants will only be able to take in the nutrients in the nutrient solution if it is at a specific pH range. To ensure this, purchase a pH meter that you shall regularly use to determine the pH of your nutrient solution.

When it comes to measuring pH levels, you will have different options. You can use test strips, a liquid kit, or an electronic meter. Electronic meters are preferred because they are inexpensive and convenient to use.

You should get a pH up and a pH down to help you in adjusting the pH of your nutrient solution. Start with a small amount of each because as you shall realize, plants tend to use nutrients that cause the solution to lean towards one direction, and you will find that you always use one and not the other. However, have both so that you can correct all the spikes and dips that could happen were there to be a nutrient lockout.

7. **Add And Mix Your Nutrients to Get Your System Going**

Once you have everything ready, it's time to get the system going. You must first get some water running in your setup, to test whether everything will work as smoothly. This step will allow you to catch any leaks that would come up. Wait it out for some minutes, at least, and if everything is still running as well as it could, mix your nutrients, let the solution rest for some 15 minutes, and then test its pH. Adjust your solution's pH if you deem it necessary.

Once that is done, set your plants on the system and set the timer of your grow light to the light duration that your plants need to grow properly.

As you can see, the process of getting your garden ready is very easy, but the key is to make preparations prior and to spend enough time planning upfront. This will save you both money and time, in the end.

Ensuring That Your Water Will Not Kill Your Plants

If you can, it is best to use Reverse Osmosis (RO) water to make your nutrient solution. Hydroponics produces the best when you invest the best. If you have already provided the best lighting, the best nutrients, the best hydroponic system, why would you skimp out and use poor water? You need great water to ensure that the plants get the most out of the solution you make. Great water simply comes from a great filtration process. Remember that water, particularly hard water contains minerals and other stuff that could knock over the balance you are seeking to achieve when it comes to your nutrients, even if you have followed the manufacturer's instructions to the letter.

There's one way to know whether your water is good enough or whether you will need reverse osmosis water. It is done by measuring the alkalinity of the water, by checking the presence of bicarbonates and carbonates. You just have to conduct a PPM test. If the results show that your water has a 10 or below PPM, you can go ahead and use your tap water. If the test shows over 10 PPM, you need to invest in a reverse osmosis system. It may surprise you to know that when such tests were conducted, some waters ended up with a 900PPM, completely choked by alkalinity. This water would be disastrous if used in hydroponics.

So, what is this reverse osmosis that is meant to reduce the nutrient concentration in alkaline water? Let's first understand what osmosis is. Osmosis is the process through which a solvent moves across a semipermeable membrane that separates two solutions of different concentration. Whenever osmosis is used to purify water, the same semipermeable membrane is used, but also a pressurized system is used to push the solvent across the membrane.

Reverse osmosis is a water purification technology that uses a semipermeable membrane to draw molecules, ions and large particles from drinking water. It can even draw out bacteria. This method is used in industries and the production of potable water. It results in the solute, in this case, dissolved nutrients, remaining on the pressurized side of the membrane while the pure water passes to the other side.

If you are using reverse osmosis to clean your water or if you are using your tap water for hydroponics farming, you need to realize that the recommended pH for most of the plants we have indicated above is somewhat low, between 5.5 and 6.3. Most tap water has a pH of between 7.0 and 8.0. Therefore, you need to purchase a testing kit to test your water, and if the pH is not within the recommended range, you will need to add, either the pH Up or the pH Down.

It is important that you be careful about the pH of your nutrient solution because if the pH gets out of the right range, which could happen very swiftly sometimes, your plants' ability to absorb secondary, macro and micronutrients, vitamins, and carbohydrates, among others, will be lowered.

The truth is that issues of pH in a hydroponics system can be a real source of headache. However, the good news is that if you take up the right products, you can eliminate all these issues and you would never have to worry about them.

Beginners Should Opt for Clones

If you are just getting into hydroponics farming, you want the process to be as seamless and as enjoyable as possible. The best way to do this is by taking out all kinds of factors that could go wrong. For this reason, it is recommended that beginners start growing their gardens from live plants, instead of using seeds. This is what is called 'cloning.'

Using the example of growing herbs, you just have to get an herb seedling, gently take it out of the soil and the potting container from which it had been growing, and wash the dirt from off the roots, so that it doesn't contaminate the water. If you leave any soil on the roots, it could lead to fungal or bacterial infestation, or even cause the roots to rot. Once you have cleaned off the roots, just add the plant into your net pot that is secured on the lid of the bucket holding the nutrient solution. Cover the roots with the growing media, and let the system take it up from there.

Preparing the Growing Media

With any of the growing media, you may choose, you will want to wash and disinfect it first before application. You need to do this before the initial application, and at each reuse. You could wash the material while it is in the grow pots, or take the easier option of washing it in a larger container so you can easily flush and drain it.

If the growing media has been used before, you need to even be more thorough in your cleaning exercise so that you get off all the previous nutrients and the old roots. Washing the material for initial application is not as tough because you only need to disinfect the growing material and to take out any dust that the media could have come with. You just need clean water for washing, don't try to use cleaners.

Disinfecting the growing medium is done using hydrogen peroxide or diluted bleach. Get the hydrogen peroxide to a 3% concentration or dilute the bleach to 10% concentration. Disinfecting the growing medium helps to protect the system from microscopic pests for which you cannot introduce a natural predator once they infect your hydroponic system. Therefore, ensure that you make an effort to ensure this for yourself, to avoid problems along the way.

Once you have prepared the disinfectant solution, dip the growing media in, and allow it to remain submerged for about an hour. When the hour lapses, now go ahead and vigorously rinse off all that disinfectant. If the media has developed mold, it would be very difficult to wash it off, and the best thing to do is to discard the growing media, and replacing it with a fresh bunch.

Coming Up with the Correct Watering Cycle for Your Plants

Make sure to test out your watering cycle before you get started with your plants. Most watering cycles have 15 minutes or more, between the cycles. Avoid having an off period of more than 30 minutes, and if you are using a slow drip system, set long watering times, like 5 or more hours, then take a 15 to 30-minute breaking interval.

Slow drip pumps take in very little power, and the long off cycles extend the pump's life. For example, a 250 gph pump can water up to 50 plants if the drip rate is at 1 gph per plant. This is not a usual rate, but still, the timer you buy will be the primary determinant and guide to your watering cycle.

Whatever timer or pump you go for, keep in mind the fact that it will serve you well to have a water application system that distributes water evenly over the surface of the growing media.

Therefore, don't just buy one or two drips and call it a day; you want to install a drip every 16 square inches, or even less, to reduce the number of dry zones in your growing media.

Once the water gets to the growing media, it will redistribute itself outward through capillary action and from there, as the water begins to drain, the entire material will be adequately moist. Keep trying for different times on your timer until you establish a timing interval that gets you the best moisture level while avoiding the intermittent dry conditions. Don't be worried about the usage of the nutrient solution because the solution that drains from the growth medium into the reservoir below will be pumped back into the material again. Therefore, the entire affair will be about ensuring a moist environment for your plants.

If you take the drip system, ensure that you install an in-line screen to take out the debris from the water and to keep the emitters from plugging or the pipe from aging. If you are using clay pellets for a medium, know that the pellets will release some particles also, and these could clog the pipes too. Also, expect the growth of algae because it naturally occurs in water, and it grows very fast particularly where nutrients are involved. Once you install the inline filter, however, you can do away with the algae also. Therefore, you need to ensure that your filter remains clean by taking it out and washing it often.

You need to take note of the fact that since the solution reservoir has both water and nutrients, it makes an ideal breeding ground for algae. The algae will reduce the efficacy of the nutrients you place in the reservoir. However, to prevent this, ensure that your reservoir tank is opaque, to prevent light passing to the algae cells that need it for their growth.

The Right Nutrition for Hydroponics

When you have just transferred your clones from the germination room to the growth tray, application of a fertilizer that has a high nitrogen content is the wrong way to go. This is because nitrogen promotes foliar growth in plants, and the primary need for the plants at that young age is to develop their root system not to have large leaves. This is to show you that the nutrients you apply to the plant will change based on the plant's growth stage.

The soil already has a considerable amount of micro and macronutrients, but in the soilless hydroponic gardening style, there will be no nutrients in the solution, unless you add them. The good thing is that it is not difficult to determine what a plant needs at a particular stage; you just have to conduct research and seek advice from experienced farmers on the needs of the plants, and how to go about meeting those needs. Once you figure this out, you will be surprised at how healthy and vigorous the growth of your plants will be.

Why Your Attention Should Remain with the Roots

In a hydroponic setup, the main determinant of health, growth, and productivity of the plants are the roots. The roots are the point of contact between the rest of the plant and the essential nutrients the plant needs to survive and make food. It is also how the plant gets water, for cooling and transportation of nutrients produced in the leaves. Therefore, there is more than a sound reason why you should maintain healthy roots, and one of the key ways to ensure that the roots remain healthy is by ensuring that they have a sufficient amount of oxygen around them.

If the roots of a plant, whether planted in the soil or at a soilless environment, suffer from low oxygen, or lack of it, the roots shrivel up, and they die.

You also need to address water stagnation with immediacy. Although a hydroponic solution can be secured in a closed reservoir, the water therein needs to be in constant movement so that it can interact with the environment. This interaction allows the exchange of gas molecules, although this can also be achieved by installing an air pump at the bottom of the reservoir, as they do in aquariums.

Another fact to keep in mind in regards to the roots is the reality of transplant shock. It occurs when the roots of a seedling, transplanted from a smaller hydroponic germination setup, die upon arrival at the main system. To avoid this, ensure that you carry out the transplanting very slowly but surely. Avoid rushing the process, and ensure that your main agenda is to keep your fragile root hairs alive.

The roots need to be kept moist for as long as the plant needs to be kept alive. However, this is not to say that the roots should be submerged in some stagnant solution.

How Does A Good Hydroponics System Look Like?

A hydroponic system can be judged by its looks: not how colorful or beautiful it looks, but by how the setup has been placed. Want to know if the setup you have looks good, here are the factors you should consider:

- The overall system design should be simple, relatively inexpensive, and easy to implement

- The maintenance costs to the owner should be almost non-existence because the setup should take care of 99% of its issues.

- The system should be fully automated and the only role the farmer plays is to test the solution content, and add to them when the need arises

- The system should be ideal and ready to house and meet the needs of the plants it was meant to house. Simply, the system should serve the purpose for which it was set up.

- There should be no wastage of the nutrient solution.

- The setup should be able to deliver the right air, water and nutrient combination to the plants so that the crops do not just survive, but they thrive in the hydroponic setup.

The Best Low-Cost and Environmental-Friendly Way to Power Your Hydroponics System

So far, you have thought about everything you need for your garden, from the water, the nutrients, the solution, the growing medium, the physical setup, lighting, and it may look like you have covered everything. However, my goal here is to ensure that your plunge into the hydroponics world is as seamless as possible.

There is one more issue we need to think about: how best can we lower the running costs? One way to do this is to lower the cost of power. How would you like to tap solar power from the sun to your garden? Fantastic idea, right? Now let's see how you should do that.

A hydroponic system demands a continuous supply of a lot of power, especially if you are operating a recirculating system to provide your plants with the necessary nutrition, and to return the excess solution back to the reservoir.

As you would expect, the most reliable power source would be if you tapped into the alternating current provided through the national grid. However, some people are keen to ensure that while their farms are running smoothly, they do not contribute to the worsening of global warming scourge.

How would a hydroponics farmer achieve this objective? He or she would tap into solar power. If you do things the right way, you can run your entire greenhouse hydroponics operations relying on solar energy alone, powering it both day and night.

For this project, you would need a car or solar battery (you are not restricted to just one), a low voltage direct current breaker, some wires of an appropriate size, solar panels (Ideally, 100 watts or more. Your power needs will dictate this), a voltage regulator, an inverter to convert direct current to alternating current, and a solar charge controller.

Here are the steps you should take to bring the above items together:

1. Securely mount your solar panels at the top of a roof, ensuring that the frames are angled appropriately, in a way that will set the panels up for maximum exposure to the sun's UV rays. Ensure that the panel is not positioned in the shade of a tree because the shade reduces the reach of the rays to your panel, thereby reducing the effectiveness of the solar setup. Do all you can to ensure maximum exposure.

2. Create the connection between the solar panels on the roof to low voltage breakers in the house. Ensure that you are connecting the right wire as you do this because setting up any electrical system, including the solar panel, can prove to be very dangerous. If you are doing this yourself, take some time to conduct thorough research before you join any wires. Otherwise, call an electrician.

Do not confuse the low voltage breakers with the normal circuit breakers though. A DC breaker is built to break short-circuits that come up when the voltages are very low while the normal AC circuit breaker breaks voltages that are very high, to restore normal functionality.

Therefore, the DC low voltage breakers you connect to the solar panels are meant to ensure that the line coming directly from the solar panel, were there to be an electrical catastrophe, will not burn the entire solar panel setup.

3. Connect the solar charge controller to the car battery or the solar battery. If you are running a hybrid solar setup, opt for a large capacity car or truck batteries. Normally, solar panels use 12-volt or 24-volt batteries, but getting a battery of a higher strength will cause it to last longer, and to provide more power in a day, compared to that given by the lower voltage batteries.

4. Now connect the batter to your DC-AC inverter. It inverts the direct current from the battery into alternating current that is used to run appliances and equipment in your garden, and even in your house.

5. The last connection of the solar setup is between the inverter and the regulator. A power regulator regulates the power going to your appliances or equipment, while also acting as a circuit breaker. In case of a short circuit, the fuse in the regulator blows, breaking the connection immediately, and protecting you and your appliances from fires that come when wires are shorted.

You can now connect the power regulator to your multi-tap power extension setup. The extension tap should be heavy-duty, and able to break the circuit in case of faults.

It is also of great importance that you get some lightning protect taps for the event your greenhouse is struck by lightning. The lightning cap should be able to turn itself on in the event there is an extreme power surge, and this will save your hydroponic equipment from electrical damage.

The setup you have created will function as follows: In the morning, your plants will be feeding off the light rays from the sun, and at the same time, your battery will be charging. When night reaches, the battery will be at a complete charge, powering the grow lights you purchases, the air pump, the submersible pump, and other systems, up until morning when your battery starts powering again.

Notice that although the pumps and timers will be running during the day, the energy they consume will be almost negligible because the battery will be continually charging.

The benefit of a solar system is that since you have installed numerous safety measures, the system can safely run on autopilot. Remember that one of the characteristics of a good hydroponic setup is that it should be able to take care of itself. Only ensure that each morning, you check the readings on different parts of the system to ensure that everything is working normally.

CHAPTER 6
Common Mistakes Hydroponics Beginners Make

Since you are just now getting into hydroponics gardening, you may want to take things as slowly and as carefully as you could. One mistake could send the entire project rolling down the hill, and no one wants that. What an investment you have made, and how sad it would be to see it all amount to nothing! What you do to prevent this is to get first, a clear understanding of what your intended plants expect of you and how to attend to each of their needs.

While knowing what to do is important, you should also beware of what not to do, because doing so would mess up your project. Below is a review of common mistakes beginner hydroponic gardeners can make:

#1: Going Cheap By Sourcing Ineffective or Not Buying Enough Lighting

Lighting can make or break your hydroponic garden. If you buy the wrong kind of bulb, your plants will suffer. The same will happen if you provide too little lighting. The growth of your plants will stunt. The cheapest bulbs too, may not perform as well as required.

One of the most critical investments you ought to make as a hydroponic farmer is to seek the best lighting for your crops. This requires you to conduct first, substantial research in the market, and among seasoned hydroponic farmers, on the right kind of lighting, bearing in mind that different bulbs will produce different kinds of energy and light spectrums.

Also, don't expect that placing your plants next to a window is enough substitution for grow lights because usually, the light that gets in through the window is not sufficient, or strong enough to support the vigorous growth common among hydroponic plants.

#2: Designing Unusable or Difficult-To-Use Hydroponic Farms

Some beginners make the mistake of designing an unusable farm because they lack experience or because they have not dealt with hydroponics before, at least not on a large scale.

Due to inexperience, they fail to think about factors like efficiency and workflow, which leads to farms that make regular maintenance operations difficult, make harvesting difficult and do not use the space available efficiently. These inefficient gardens may also demand lots of tending, transplanting due to death of the plants, and difficulties controlling pests. Farmers also have a difficult time accessing various parts of the systems.

Now that labor is the most expensive variable cost in a farm, it is of great importance that the farms have labor-efficient designs.

The solution to this mistake is to take some considerable time to plan out and think about how the system will work, and from there, you can now build individual components. Consider all the variables, including water, nutrients, light, pests, convenience, access, redundancy, and automation, right from the start, and only start planning out the design once you have figured out each of the variables mentioned.

It would help if you went benchmarking, by visiting and talking to seasoned growers to see the systems they are operating. Go ahead and ask questions, including seeking answers to the question of what they would do differently were they to turn back and begin afresh.

#3: Confusing Biological Viability with Economic Viability

One of the misconceptions flying around the agricultural product markets is that establishing a farm requires 90% growing while selling takes 10%. However, when it comes to reality, the opposite is true, and many farmers make mistakes on either of the systems.

The farmers fail to take into consideration the financial costs and the time it would take for them to get their produce to the market once it has matured, and because of this small omission, many do not budget either money or the time that they would need to get their produce to the consumers. This effectively disrupts the schedule they had previously set for the farm and can lead to frustration due to lack of a market.

The second batch are those that go-ahead to plan for the biological functions of their farms, including the crops to grow, the techniques to use, and the equipment to source for, but they do all this without testing the feasibility of what they are producing in the market. They are not careful to ensure that what they are producing matches the local demand. In the end, the farmers are frustrated at having a lot of produce and a facility, with no consumers to buy what they have grown.

The bottom line is that it will not matter how much effort you have dedicated to your farm, or how healthy and better tasting they are if no one wants them.

#4: Underestimating the Cost of Crop Production and Of Purchasing the Hydroponic System

It is typical of many motivated and determined hydroponic beginners to be so excited about getting into the hydroponic business that they underestimate just how they would have to spend to succeed at it. Beginners are often asked to start small and scale to bigger establishments with time, even if they feel like they have the resources they would need to go big. The problem is that some do not heed this instruction, and instead, they enter the industry and purchase large facilities, equipment, and expensive utilities.

Unfortunately, those who go ahead to start their gardens find that the costs of running hydroponic gardens are way too high, and some may quit in the middle of it due to the inadequacy of resources. Others do not even get to start the production process because by the time they finish purchasing the equipment and other resources, they no longer have any money to move ahead. The result is that in either case, the farmers do not get the chance to utilize their equipment fully due to unanticipated costs.

Therefore, as you make plans for your intended project, keep in mind costs like pest control, heat removal, replacement of equipment, labor, insurance, packaging, ongoing maintenance, and the cost of printing marketing materials. All these costs add up to a significant amount.

The most critical of the costs that are often underestimated is the cost of labor, whether the farmer is providing it himself or hiring someone to do it. If you are producing in rafts, for example, realize that it is a labor-intensive hydroponic production practice. The cost of labor for raft systems can go up to 45% or 60% of the total production costs. Many producers do not even take notice of this when calculating and making their estimates. Therefore, when they get to the harvesting and processing stages, they are left in shock, not believing what their returns have become.

#5: Choosing the Wrong Market

The market for which you are producing is another critical factor that you ought to consider, whether your project is producing food to be sold later, or to be consumed by your family. If you grow crops that your market does not want, you will be wasting resources and opportunity. The result is that you will be trying to push your products on unwilling consumers, leading to wastage, and a loss of resources because you will not get a return on your investment.

Some crops are easy to grow, and when they are grown under hydroponics, their production is especially high. However, the crops are just unwanted. Therefore, before you decide on the crop you want to grow, conduct a proper analysis of your market, and even so, look at what your competition is growing. From there, come up with something that will give you lots of customers.

If you are living in an area where field producers present fierce competition with their produce, choose to produce what the producers cannot grow in that period. In most cases, if a consumer, say a restaurant, wants to buy organic lettuce and the field producer offers it at 50 cents a pound, the field producer will have the attention of the consumer, at least for the summer period, when he is producing.

When the seasonal competition is too stiff, come up with ways to survive and not lose your spot in the market. If you prove to be reliable, you will win the loyalty of many consumers, and you can lock them into permanent purchasing contracts, such that they will not even consider other producers, cheaper or not.

The bottom line here is that you should choose a crop whose market is guaranteed.

#6: Choosing Hydroponic Systems That Have Poor Reputations, Then Expecting Different Results

When you are trying to choose the right system to implement, do not be so focused on the project's supposed profitability. Get some reliable information from system users on the experiences they had using the system. If you do not know any, ask your sellers to lead you to someone that has used the system for a while, and if the sellers cannot do this, walk away. If you get to see some referees, be careful to find out whether their systems are profitable or not.

#7: Choosing the Wrong Crop for Your Setup and Climate

The marketing language being used in most seed catalogs is filled with beautiful descriptions, and it is easy for a producer to be seduced into growing some exotic crops that are not suited to his hydroponic system or to his climate. In addition, the crops might not even be in demand in his local market.

Before you settle on a particular streak of crop for your project, consider some important factors. Consider the constraints that your environment could have placed on you, the growing technique you will take up, and whether the crop is suited to the production technique you have settled for.

Kindly note that different crops will have different needs, and some can only be grown in a particular, specified way. For example, those that are using rafts should not consider growing tomatoes. In the same way, growers who use granite as the growing medium should not expect to reap worthwhile root crops.

You need to put a lot of thought into your production decisions. If you live in the southern hemisphere and are constantly battling heat, your attempts to grow cool weather crops like rhubarb will be a poor decision. If you live in the Northern hemisphere and you want to grow crops with a long day length, the eight-hour day will not work well for you there.

#8: Becoming Too Big, Too Fast

Surprisingly, this is a common mistake among hydroponic growers. Some growers will go and look for funding to establish some big expensive facilities even before they understand the market they are trying to get into, and the cost structure of the entire production process. Growers that take this road tend to have more catastrophic failures, and they have them more often than not.

When a big project sinks, a lot of money and other resources go down too. Even more, failure leads to supply gaps for customers who need consistent product delivery. Whenever you do not deliver, the customers will go ahead and source for a different supplier, and by the time the food producer is back to the system, he will have lost many of his customers.

You need to be patient, and to understand the growth process. Once you are not in a hurry, you have time to look around the market, identify needs you can meet, and even source for the best production resources like seeds, and fertilizers. You are also likely to get good bargains, which would considerably reduce your production costs. Observe how large entrants flood the market with new products and see how they end up with mixed results. Learn from their experiences, and avoid getting losses like those yourself.

You can do three critical things to avoid the pain of growing very fast. First, develop a niche market. Secondly, become creative in what you do, and ensure that you are offering value to your consumers. Thirdly, do not submit to the desire of overwhelming your market. With that, you will move at a reasonable pace, acquiring all the lessons you need along the way, from your experience, and that of other growers.

#9: Pulling Leaves off Your Plants

Leaves are the plants' factories, where all the sugar production takes place. This sugar is critical for all plant processes including growth and flowering. Therefore, no matter what anyone says to you, refrain from getting the leaves off your plants. Although some say that taking some leaves off induces a growth stress response that helps to reduce stretching, the practice can be detrimental to growth, and it would just be better if you left it for when you are more advanced.

#10: Getting Into the Grow Room When the Lights Are Off

When you have just started your hydroponics gardening project, you will feel like a new parent, with the urge of wanting to check on your 'baby' every so often. Some check on their plants for up to 50 times a day, and this is not good. Save your inspection for when the lights come back on.

#11: Failure to Double Check That Your Equipment Is Running Correctly

If you forget to check whether your meters are calibrated and working correctly, fail to plug in your pumps and fail to check whether your timers have been set and are working correctly, you could fall into a whole lot of problems. Therefore, you need to check, and keep rechecking your equipment, and its settings.

#12: Using Unreliable Equipment to Conduct Very Important Tasks

We already mentioned that you should avoid cheap, inefficient lighting, but the same rule applies to other equipment like fans, and timers. Although you may be working on a budget now and may need to shop on price, ensure that once you have saved up some money, you get better quality equipment. If the quality of your equipment is good, you can rely on it, you will experience fewer equipment failures, and you will have safer gear that does not tear and wear easily.

#13: Adding Nutrients and Water Every Time You Top Up Your Nutrient Solution

This is mostly done by gardeners who are using tap water for their farms. Tap water already has some salt in it, and when you add some salt to it, in the form of the fertilizer you introduce, the nutrients will be taken up in varying ratios. Whenever you want to increase your solution, you add some water, and when you do this, you introduce some new salts into the solution, which could introduce a nutrient imbalance because the plant food may become so concentrated. An imbalance can harm or even burn the plants.

If you insist on tap water, you would be better off just adding water to your solution, without having to add any nutrients, until the nutrient salts reach desirable levels as indicated by the EC meter. In a number of days, when the liquid level in your tank will get lower, you may dump the current solution and refill your tank with a new batch. Ensure that the solution level is high because as experienced gardeners will tell you, particularly those that use recycling systems, the higher the solution level, the better. In addition, the more frequently you dump out your used solution, the better it is for your crops.

The bottom line is that when you add water, just add it up to the point where the salt ratios in the solution are maintained, at the most desirable levels.

#14: Failing to Take In Important Lessons As You Go

Parents talk of each of their children as different, despite having the same gene pool. Identical twins, despite being similar in appearance, will have unique characteristics. This is the case for all crops you will be rearing in your hydroponic system. You may plant the same crops you did the previous round and be surprised that there are problems with the current one, or the yields are different.

It is likely that you missed a step, did not mix the nutrient solution as you did previously, and other changes you may have effected. Take some time to compare and analyze the two growing periods, and see how you can adjust your practices for the next crops.

The best way to keep tabs on what you did in a particular crop cycle is to photograph, document and take note of all the bad and the good aspects of the system you have and the crops you planted. Whenever you have mapped out the problem, it is easier to keep thinking, and eventually finding a solution to your problems. Conduct research from websites, books, and the all-friendly YouTube, and you will find all kinds of solutions lined up.

#15: Failing To Take Note of the PH

One of the most critical yet often overlooked factors in hydroponic farming, particularly among beginners, is the pH issue. Plants are only able to take in particular minerals at specified pH levels. As stated earlier, hydroponics gardens tend to maintain a pH of between 5.5 and 6, because it is at this slightly acidic environment that plants are able to take in the right nutrients.

You need to have a pH meter with you so that you can measure the content of your nutrient solution more often, and when it doesn't fall in the recommended range, make adjustments accordingly. Monitor the pH at least once every day, as this is one of the most common reasons plants die, and since they are using the same solution if one is affected, they all are, and they all die.

#16: Failing To Learn

The hydroponics idea has been in existence since early on in the 20th century, and in that time, much research and learning has taken place, both formal and informal. Most people then transfer the lessons they have learned into information that they place in books while others offer training seminars. All this information is helpful and you can get it either by taking up courses or reading books. It would be wise if you did both: learning from experienced farmers and reading books. There are also regular updates on the internet, and these too will inform you of new developments in the practice, technology advancements and of changes in the market.

Whatever you do, don't get into hydroponics gardening alone. Even if you feel like you already know everything, there is always something you ought to learn. Share ideas with other hydroponic gardeners and get to know what they have been up to. The more knowledge you gather before making your first move, the more prepared you will be, the smoother the journey will be, and the more fulfilling your harvest will be.

#17: Giving Your Plants the Wrong Food

Sometimes, it will feel like it would not hurt too much if you just picked a sack of fertilizer from your local store and feed your plants before you accessed the right one. After all, the regular fertilizer contains the nutrients that your plants need too, right? Wrong.

Regular fertilizer may fail to dilute all the way and may clog the tubes and drains of your system. Instead, opt for the kind of fertilizer specially designed for hydroponic systems. The right kind will be in liquid form or granules. It is in the right concentration and will meet the needs of your plants have in their soilless environment. It will provide all the nutrients your plants need.

#18: Failing To Keep Your Garden Clean

If you are used to throwing stuff in your soil garden with the assurance that it will decompose, don't try that with a hydroponic garden. Your garden area is not a garbage bin, and the critical issue is that the level of hygiene you uphold will affect the flow of your hydroponic system and on your plants' health.

To ensure that your garden is in proper hygiene conditions, keep your floor dry and clean, sterilize your cleaning tools, and dispose of all plant waste. Sterilize and clean the entire system when you can, and don't forget to clean the containers holding the nutrient solution.

If you do not ensure proper sanitation, you could provide breeding and hiding spaces for pests, and encourage the spread of crop diseases.

#19: Failing To Ensure Proper Oxygen Flow

Most beginners assume that plants only need carbon dioxide to survive and therefore do not attend to the oxygen needs of their plants. The truth is that plant roots need access to oxygen to aid respiration. If the roots are not healthy, they become susceptible to disease and pathogens that cause rotting of the roots. However, the more the plant is able to access oxygen, the better it is for the plant and the farmer.

Some hydroponic systems do not require you to pump in oxygen into the nutrient solution because oxygen infuses into them just by how they operate. A good example would be an ebb and flow system that drains its excess nutrient solution down the grow bed, and in the process, allows the roots to be exposed to air. Other systems like the deep-water culture system require an air pump and an air stone to help oxygenate the nutrient solution. In the deep-water culture system particularly, ensure that you use at least more than one air stone.

#20: Failing To Regulate Temperature

Most often, beginners do not remember that the temperatures of the germination room and the grow room should be regulated. In addition, some will focus on the temperature of the room and forget to check the temperature of the nutrient solution.

Whenever the temperature of the solution rises, the air is continually bubbled out of the solution, which means that as temperature rises, the amount of dissolved oxygen keeps going down. A low oxygen volume affects the health of the roots and boosts the development and growth of pathogens. Therefore, ensure that the solution maintains a temperature of between 65 and 75 F. degrees.

The temperature of the air is also critical for different developmental stages of the plant. For seeds, if the temperature is too low or too high, the seeds can't germinate. This is the same case for fruit and flower production. General plant growth will also be affected. For example, if veggies like broccoli and lettuce are kept in a very hot environment, they begin to bolt. Therefore, for a maximum harvest, ensure that you stick to the recommended plant temperatures.

#21: A Lack of Understanding of Hydroponic Nutrients

Hydroponic solutions are not just about parts and mixing ratios; care must be taken to ensure that the plants are getting the right nutrients for their growth stage, plant type, and the contents of the fertilizers. To begin with, realize that plants need varying ratios of N-P-K nutrients depending on their growth stage. For example, at the vegetative stage, plants will require a high amount of nitrogen while flowering plants need more potassium and phosphorus.

The market is flooded with different fertilizers with varying nutrients ratios, but before you make a purchase, you ought to conduct first, a study of what your plant needs to ensure that you are providing proper nutrients, at the right stage, so that it can reach its full potential.

#22: Inadequate Circulation for Your Garden

When a growing space is warm and humid, there arises the potential for mold growth in your hydroponic garden. To reduce this risk, you need to ensure proper air circulation by including a fan or installing a proper air conditioning system that lets out the hot air and brings in some cool air. In the event your garden is fully enclosed, consider adding some vents to allow fresh air in. This air exchange keeps the temperatures of the place down. Therefore, as a hydroponics beginner, ensure that you do not overlook the issue of circulation through increased ventilation.

CHAPTER 7
Useful Tips for Hydroponic Farming

If you review any of the hydroponic farming tips, given in this topic, you may see that the tips center on three primary issues, which are: lack of knowledge, lack of discipline and inability. People lack an understanding of what should be and the things they need to do to see it through. Others know what is expected of them but do not care enough to put in the time and effort to see it through. The third category is of people who do not have the proper hydroponic equipment or lack proper knowledge of how to run activities on a hydroponic farm.

However, the tips that this chapter provides will give you the necessary knowledge to help you identify and avoid having any of the three issues mentioned, in your garden. While you may make some mistakes here and there, having foreknowledge of what to expect and the tricks to take up to reach your goal sooner and help you achieve greater success in what you do.

The tips you should keep in mind include:

1) Always have a plan

It is impossible to run a hydroponics garden and be successful at it without a plan. What to include in your plan is the nutritional needs of your plants, the light or photoperiod, the equipment you need to operate, how to meet the labor needs at the garden, and how to access the nutrients that your plants need.

You should actually have a week-by-week plan of what to do, and you should incorporate information about the nutrient changes to have and other important information. Some nutrient kits come with this information, but some packages will require you to consult a professional or an experienced farmer.

2) Prioritize the health of the roots

Damaged roots will paralyze the entire plant because they are unable to take up the required nutrients to the plant. Therefore, in case there is damage at the bottom, expect the same damage at the top, in the form of sick plants, wilting plants, and damaged leaves.

The way to protect your roots is by ensuring that your solution is at the right concentration, uncontaminated and aerated. You need two solution reservoirs, one to contain the water you will be using when you discard the current solution when 14 days lapse. The second precaution is putting in measures to reduce your solution's exposure to light. This is helpful because it prevents algae growth, which in turn prevent the formation of fungus gnats that cause most of the plant root problems.

3) Temperature control

One of the most critical tips in hydroponic farming is temperature control. Since hydroponic farming takes place in an enclosed humid location, a greenhouse or a house, the temperature can rise quickly, and when it gets to 85 degrees, plant growth stops, unless you install a pump that raises the CO_2 concentration in the room.

When using artificial lighting to grow the crops, especially the lights themselves will emit substantial heat that can become a problem for your in house garden. It could help if you found a way to place your light's ballast outside the grow room unless of course, you have the digital kind of ballast that does not emit heat. Since you need these lights, invest in something that will bring in some cold air, and note that fans are not an adequate measure.

4) You need to provide proper, adequate lighting

When it comes to bringing light to an indoor garden, you have a few options. At a minimum, you need to provide 40 to 60 watts lighting per square foot. The best choices in the market to help you bring this to life include the metal halide lights or the high-pressure sodium lights. The two are the most popular choices among farmers.

You need to know that when it comes to fluorescent lighting, regular fluorescent lights do not provide enough lighting to support healthy growth. This kind of lighting is only good for seedlings, clones, and plants that are very young, and in their vegetative stage like the spinach, kitchen herbs, and lettuce.

For your grow room, opt for T5 lights, also called Tek lights because they emit less heat in comparison to HID lights, and they use less energy. Ensure that your plants are only a few inches away from the lights. The lights should be overhead the plants.

5) Feeding or nutrition tips

Before you make any steps, such as deciding on the setup, the location and other details, conduct research to determine the nutritional needs of your intended crops. Take note of the expected strength of the concentration for each week of the plant's life, take note of the names of the fertilizers you will need and from where you will source them.

For example, most plants need a high amount of nitrogen in their infancy (not as young as clones) and then switch to needing high phosphorus amounts once they begin to flower and produce fruits. To ensure that you are kept abreast about the strength of your nutrient solution, ensure that you get yourself an EC meter or a TDS meter, and adjust the solution as the plants develop, moving from one stage to the next.

As a beginner, do not attempt to mix up your own plant solution, opt for the professionally made hydroponics nutrients concentrate. It is a three-part fertilizer, and it is easy to use. Once you have gotten used to the system and have had success producing crops, perhaps after you have recovered your cost of setup (for business persons), then you can try making your own nutrient solution, and observing how the plants respond to every change you make. If things are not working out, at least you will know exactly what the issue is, and you can make adjustments.

The same is the case for any additives. As a beginner, stay away from solutions said to improve your farm results. This issue is an especially common problem among beginner farmers who are anxious for the big results. Instead, farmers should work with the three-part nutrients first, because they are good enough and adequate for the plants, and they should postpone any plans to boost production until when their systems begin to work smoothly and to produce good results. Then you can add liquid seaweed, vitamin B1, Silica, or a combination of the three.

Another critical thing is on your need to check the nutrient solution reservoir every single day. We have already established that the nutrient solution ought to be changed every 14 days.

6) Your choice of growing medium is of absolute importance

The growing media is the core of your farming, and you need to realize that it is expensive, requires labor, and needs space. It provides support to your crops. With these considerations, you need to realize that it is only by choosing the right medium that your work will be made easier while choosing the wrong one will bring setbacks and speed bumps to your development.

Therefore, you need to arm yourself with some tips that have to do with the specific growing medium. They include:

a. You need to appreciate the process and the technique of using your specific medium

Each medium is different, and just because it worked out great for one person, it doesn't have to work out the same for another farmer. However, you need to have studied all there is to know about the medium you have chosen so that you know how, when and where to use it.

For example, coconut coir is good for systems for which you do not have to be concerned about the medium disintegrating or being washed through the system. It does not work well in systems where it will be handled heavily. Rockwool is not suited for systems where it would also be compressed. However, polymer-bound plugs are suitable for systems in which they would be compressed.

b. Be sure to ask the right questions

You need to know all there is about your hydroponic system and process, but some questions are more critical than others. You need to know how much you and your laborers will be handling the growing material, find out if the material is suited for automation and whether the medium will compress during the handling process or in the equipment. See also, whether you will be required to dispose of the medium, or whether you can re-use it.

c. Make an estimate of the external costs

Choosing a cheap medium ignores the cost of maintaining the product, especially in regard to the labor, germination requirements, and the issues of disposal. Know the external costs that come with your medium, and find out whether it may require any kind of special treatment from the germination, planting, growing and harvesting process.

d. Take into consideration the unique needs that come with particular growing material such as the structure of the hydroponic system, aeration, or the shear strength of the material.

e. Consider all factors present before making your decision.

Once you have known all there is to know about your growing media, learn how it will interact with the rest of the farm. Bring all the knowledge you have been collecting in regards to the hydroponic garden, and with careful consideration, go ahead and make your decision. Consider the certification objectives, conditions for germination, irrigation strategies, crop size, price, and automation goals.

7) The Process of Germinating Your Seed

There are many ways you could employ to germinate your seeds. They include:

a. Pre-soaking
In this method, the farmer puts some moist tissues on a plate, then places his seeds on top of the tissues. He then places another layer of wet tissues on the seeds and covers the plate with another

upturned plate. The seeds remain in the dark space that has been created, and their environment remains moist due to lack of exposure to the air and the elements of the environment. Ensure that the place in which the seeds remain is warm, about 21 degrees Celsius.

Ensure that you check on your seeds every day and wet the tissues when the moisture in them begins to dry out. Once the seeds are germinated, carefully transplant them. The skin should have broken, and the tip of the root should be visible. Now, place the germinated seed on the growing medium, ensuring that it is approximately 5 mm from the surface.

b. Using the growing medium to germinate seeds

You could still germinate your seeds in the growing medium. You only have to place the seeds about 5mm under the surface, then regularly sprinkle the growth medium with some water, ensuring that it does not get too wet. The seed germinates and uses the food stored in its cotyledons to germinate and grow. At this point, the air is a critical component because it provides the oxygen needed for metabolism. Therefore, ensure that the medium remains somewhat airy by ensuring that it is not standing in the water and that it is able to drain properly when excess liquid is sprinkled on it.

c. Growing the plants outside
Although hydroponics is about growing your crops in a soilless environment, sometimes it helps to ask for help from the soil (pun intended). Since germinating seeds indoors takes a much shorter time than when you do it outdoors, farmers can take up hydroponics for the germination of their seeds before they transfer them to the fields. This method is also ideal because usually, the ground temperature is not ideal between the months of April and May. Only put out the emerged seedlings outside, at a place where they can start to learn how to get used to the outdoor environment.

8) Caring for the young seedlings

Since the newly emerged plants from the seedlings are still quite delicate, ensure that you do not place them under a 400-watt lamp, and if using natural light, do not place them directly in the sun because they could burn. Only work on providing your plants with water containing nutrients to help them build and strengthen their roots system.

9) Get Proper Tools and Equipment

Unless you have figured out all details in regards to the tools and equipment you need, and how to properly use each of them, do not take any step towards starting your garden. For this, you will need a high-powered fan, a thermometer, an air conditioner, an oscillating fan, a digital timer, an extremely dark area, hydroponic gardening system, adequate lighting and other tools mentioned in a previous chapter. Each of the tools and equipment should be used with diligence and knowledge so that each serves its purpose, and to avoid any accidents or injuries.

10) Manipulate the light period

Most crops require a short daylight period to be able to get to the fruiting or flowering stage. However, consistency is key. You need to ensure a consistent on and off time for the lights, each day.

In addition, you also ought to ensure that when plants are in their dark period, they are left in complete, utter darkness for that period, without even a streak of light interrupting it. For this reason, consider getting yourself a blacked-out grow room or tent. Plants are extremely sensitive to the schedule you set, so avoid skirting around the lighting issue.

11) Clean the hydroponic system regularly

While all the steps and tips can be implemented to the letter, if the hydroponic system itself is contaminated and dirty, the effort you put into it will be reduced to naught. The system needs to be cleaned regularly to ensure its successful operation, and to keep off pests and disease.

Once you have finished sterilizing the grow room, move over to the solution reservoir. Do this by emptying the reservoir, filling it halfway, then using diluted bleach, clean it, and ensure there are no solid materials built up in the system's tubing. You could also reduce clogging by opening the system valves a few seconds each week. Once you have done that, now clean the grow buckets or trays to avoid the buildup of pathogens. The cleaning process is quite simple, and you only need the liquid containing dilute bleach and a scrubber. Do the scrub some several times, to ensure that the items are spotless, and then rinse them out with distilled water to carry away all nutrients or bleach deposits. Do this at the end of every harvest, or before the start of another growing season.

12) Take note of nutrient deficiencies in your plants

i. If a plant is lacking phosphorus, the entire plant turns bluish-green and may develop a purplish or red cast. You may also notice the lower leaves turn yellow, and the plant could start drying and adopting a greenish-brown color before it finally becomes black. A plant like this will often have stunted growth.

ii. If a plant has a potassium deficiency, its leaves will have a papery appearance and the edges of its leaves will have some dead areas. The plant's growth will also be stunted.

iii. An entire plant taking up a light green color and its lower leaves becoming yellow provides evidence of a nitrogen deficiency. Its growth also becomes stunted.

iv. When you notice that your plant's young stems and young leaves are falling off and dying, it is a sign that the plant itself is calcium deficient.

v. If the leaf tissue of your plants takes up a yellow appearance, but the veins on the leaves remain green, the plant lacks iron.

vi. If you notice that the lower leaves of your plant have turned yellow along the margin, the tips, and between the veins and that the lower leaves have wilted, know that your plant is suffering from magnesium deficiency.

vii. If the led tissue between the veins takes up a lighter color, yellow, and takes a papery appearance, know that the plant as a zinc deficiency.

viii. If you notice that the leaves of your plant have stunted, take a pale green color and they are malformed, it is likely that they lack Molybdenum.

ix. Scorched leaf tips and margins of young plants indicate boron deficiency.

x. If your young plants' leaves turn pale green but the older leaves are still green, and you notice that the plant is spindly and stunted, know that the plant is sulfur deficient.

xi. If the plant's growth has stunted, and the lower leaves have taken up a checkered pattern of green and yellow, know that they lack manganese.

xii. If the edges of your leaves appear blue or dark green, and the edges of the leaves curl upward, with the young leaves wilting permanently, know that your crops are lacking copper.

13) Taking note of powdery mildew

One of the most common fungal diseases affecting many plants is powdery mildew, also called mycelium. The fungus appears as a powder or a fuzzy white that coats the stems, leaves, and flowers. If the fungus is left unchecked, it could cause serious damage. Therefore, ensure that you take preventative steps to prevent the mildew onset, knowing that it thrives in damp, cool and poorly ventilated grow room. Therefore, opt to take preventative steps, first by ensuring that there is a clean flow of air in the growth room.

Natural cures and preventative measures for powdery mildew

a. *Using Epsom salt and baking soda*

This is both a cure and a preventative approach. You need to add three-quarters of a teaspoon of Epsom salt to a quarter teaspoon baking soda, and then add the mixture to a liter of water to come up with a solution. Once the solutions are mixed well, foliar spray on your plants generously, and then wash the solution off after a day or two, with misting water.

Please take note of the fact that because the solution you spray will contain salts, it will leave a powdery haze on your leaves, just as the mildew did. However, this will come off with time.

b. *The organic whole milk remedy*

This is a preventative method. The solution you need for it is prepared by diluting 10 parts water with one part organic whole milk. Spray this solution generously on your plants, and after a day or two, wash it off thoroughly to prevent the milk from going bad and causing an awful sour smell. Avoid spraying this solution when plants are in their flowering stage.

The dilute organic milk method is so effective that just a single treatment is enough. Kindly note that you should only use organic unpasteurized whole milk.

Here is a compilation of some quick facts and everyday practice tips to ensure that your plants grow just as anticipated:

- Ensure that you have all the equipment you would need for your hydroponic garden at home before you begin setting it up.

- Once you pick a location and leave your hydroponic system there, do not move the plants to a different location once they have adapted to their current environment

- Everything about your project must be done in a routine, from the feeding, exposure to light, dark times, and others. Plants tend to be very sensitive to their conditions, and if you allow them to work on a schedule, they will make the best of the time they have.

- Avoid walking into your garden after visiting another person's garden or having been outdoors. Only enter the garden once you have had a shower and changed your clothes.

- Ensure that anyone who intends to visit your garden follows the same protocol

- Ensure that you change your nutrients and your water every two weeks

- Clean and disinfect the entire system between crops. In addition, if your plants look discolored, stunt and unhealthy, get your pH kit and check the pH of your solution. If the pH level is just right, flush the entire hydroponic system with a detoxifying solution, such as Clearex.

- Quarantine all the new plants for 14 days before you take them to the growing room

- Keep your pets away from the garden

- Ensure that you install a filter or screen over the exhaust and the air intake

- Take note of all the equipment you will need, and realize the use of each

- Take note of all the nutritional needs of your plant

- Always use a three-part hydroponic nutrients fertilizer
- For your first attempt, avoid additional nutrient additives

- Take note of the light period your plants need

- Put down on paper, the feeding schedule of your plants even before you start your hydroponics project

- Ensure that the ballast of your lights is stored in a different room.

- Maximize the amount of exposure your plants get to the nutrient solution

- Check and regulate the nutrient concentration in your reservoir every day

- Minimize the light exposure of your fluid in the pipes and in the reservoir

- Control the dark periods using a digital timer

- Always have a reservoir of clean plain water in readiness for the next time you change nutrients

- The temperature of your solution in the reservoir should remain between 65 and 75 degrees. Use a water heater or a chiller to adjust temperature changes.

CHAPTER 8
New Developments in Hydroponics Gardening

Just like other high-tech fields, the hydroponic industry evolves constantly. We are continuously becoming aware of different plant physiology concepts, and in turn, scientists and farmers alike, are continually coming up with advanced techniques and technological developments for hydroponics. Serious farmers do not just wait for technology to advance, they are constantly thinking about how they can make their gardens more reproductive and efficient. Although it would be impossible to know where hydroponics gardening will be in the future, we can look at some of the recent gardening practices and scientific advancements to see where hydroponics gardening is headed.

In the next 50 to 60 years, hydroponics farming is likely to be the top agricultural method in use due to the increasing rate of soil degradation. In addition, as the population rises, hydroponics is likely to be the only means to grow food that can keep up with the food demands of the day. Some of the changes happening include:

New Developments in Lighting

The lighting system is at the heart of hydroponic gardening, and over the last 10 years, the advancements that have been made in regards to lighting have been astounding. For example, High-Intensity Discharge (HID) lighting is continuously being improved to increase its efficiency. Even more, double-ended lighting is increasingly becoming popular because of the advantages it offers, over and above that of standard HID lighting, such as longevity and high efficiency.

Sulphur primary lighting is also becoming increasingly popular for indoor gardens because of its unique spectral output. This is an excellent source of lighting, but what puts off gardeners is its high price. However, as manufacturing technology advances, it is expected that sulphur primary lighting will become cheaper, and more farmers will be able to afford it.

Although LED lighting has been here a while, its ability to give off customized, specific light spectrums that directly meet the needs of certain kinds of plants puts these lights ahead of other lighting technologies in terms of their potential. LED lights have been useful to the horticulture and hydroponics industries because they consume very little energy, have a long life, and are efficient.

Improvements Made on the Hydroponic Nutrients

There have been great advancements when it comes to hydroponic nutrients. For example, we can already see the rise of new specialty nutrients that 'self-buffer' to get to the desired pH. It is likely that there will be more of the self-buffering kind, some fully soluble ones that are able to maintain constant pH and ppm levels, and some time-release nutrients. The manufacturers are getting better at mixing various compounds and elements, to come up with a stable one-part formula. It is likely that the variety of one-part nutrients in the market will rise, even as we see an increase in the number of beginner gardeners dipping their feet into the pool of hydroponics.

The Rise of Micro Growing of Microgreens

As hydroponic technology continues to advance, we expect to see changes also, in the development and advancement of automated hydroponic systems used for growing microgreens like sprouts, and they will become more popular. We will still see much of the systems being used for growing grasses and microgreens because an increasing number of farmers are building hydroponic systems to grow fodder for their livestock. The systems they are using are not only affordable; they are also a source of superior food for livestock.

Increased Vertical Growing

Essentially, a hydroponic system serves the purpose of delivering nutrients. However, the vertical growing style is revolutionizing hydroponic gardens immensely by increasing the production capacity of every available space. This is due to the development of vertical gardening, which appears to be the perfect solution for dense urban area gardens because the space available there is limited. In fact, there are even vertical gardens being developed on the sides of buildings or other structures, and this trend is likely to increase in popularity.

We are also likely to see an increase in the establishment of hybrid systems, those that seek to combine the benefits of different hydroponic systems. There are likely to be more systems increasing or maximizing the delivery of oxygen to the roots and those delivering nutrients to the roots, both of which are expected to continue to shape up the future of hydroponics.

Good news to the gardeners is that in the future, they will not have to move from one store to another looking for the tools they need in their farms, because we expect an emergence of more kits that will contain everything that a gardener would need to start working on his project, including the proper nutrients and lighting. Already, these setups are quite popular, but they will become even more popular as more people begin to pick up hydroponics farming and practice it for the first time.

We also look forward to the establishment of more self-contained hydroponics gardens built into the kitchens. These gardens will be plumbed in, hard-wired, and made to look just like a dishwasher. More people now realize that it is beneficial to grow their own food, which means that the demand for the self-contained hydroponics gardens is likely to go up.

Combination of Aeroponics and Hydroponics

In 2016, a hydroponics farm, Preferred Produce, in Deming, New Mexico patented a new technology that would bring together aeroponics and hydroponics. In the new setup, tubes would be run through the hydroponic growing containers, and they would take the role of ferrying oxygen directly to the roots of the plants. The project's founder, Matthew Stong, said that the idea came from understanding that submerging the plants in water restricts their oxygen supply.

The growing of tomatoes, strawberries and bell peppers was used to test the new system, and the agriculturalists reported that the harvests were quicker and heavier than when other techniques were used. The new system proved to be a sure bet for cutting your plants' harvest time. For example, Stong was able to grow evergreen strawberries, that would usually take four months before the first harvest, and he was able to get pounds of the fruit in only two months.

Combination of Hydroponics and Soil Gardening

The Mittleider Grow Box is a relatively new concept invented by Jacob Mittleider. It combines hydroponics and soil gardening, as a way to grow the vegetable you wish to grow, even when your soil is of poor quality. Mittleider felt that although hydroponics can be used to provide the plants with all the necessary nutrients, there still will be some nutrients or elements that the soil especially contains, but we have not been able to identify it.

The method Mittleider suggests involves anchoring plants in a growing medium while they are yet held in the grow box, which helps roots to penetrate down to the soil so that they are able to access 'the best of both' media. The grow box should be at least 8 inches high and can be of any length and width, without a bottom. Identify your desired gardening spot, fill the box with sand, perlite, peat moss, and sawdust. It does not matter what you will use as your medium; you only have to ensure that it is well aerated and that it drains properly. Now did down into the soil, about an inch deep.

Now, plant your seedlings in the growing medium and cover the top of the box with material like wood chips, which are meant to keep the medium from drying too quickly, now that it is exposed to the elements of weather. Work towards watering your plants with the hydroponic nutrient solution and occasionally, apply some bit of commercial garden fertilizer at the base of the plants.

When carrying this out, as a general concept, you might want to place your plants at half the recommended distance apart that which is suggested for soil gardening. Also, be careful to ensure that the garden fertilizer you apply to the base of the plants is an exact measure of the recommended amount, to avoid burning the roots of the plants, and killing them.

The Advantages

- The Mittleider method is of benefit in the following ways:

- It is a combination of soil gardening and hydroponic principles, and this increases the yields collected from the crops.

- It is inexpensive

- The method is ideal for areas where the soil is too poor to support soil gardening by itself

- Farmers can grow their crops using growing medium made from local material like smashed rocks

- You could place a Mittleider Box anywhere, on the driveway, at a flowerbed, and other areas that would be unsuitable for conventional gardening.

Changes in the Sphere of Commercial Hydroponics

In the last decade or more, strawberries, lettuce, tomatoes, peppers, cucumbers, and cut flowers have made the bulk of commercial hydroponic crops in parts of the world where they are grown. However, of late, farmers have taken to growing rate herbs, plants that produce essential oils, Chinese vegetables and medicinal plants. Others are also growing wasabi and gourmet potatoes. There is also a growing movement that craze of growing plants for nutraceutical and pharmaceutical use. It would seem that it is now possible to grow any crop for commercial purposes via hydroponics.

There is an increasing interest in the production of salad crops and cut herbs, driven by the demand for the proximity to healthy food. The primary benefit of hydroponics is that it produces the best quality results, increasing its competitiveness in the market, over cheaper quality crops. For example, it produces the most superbly favored tomatoes, and potatoes. In time, we expect to see an increase in the demand for edible flowers, those that particularly used in hotel complexes and restaurants. In truth, there are now very few crops that cannot be grown hydroponically, and the only factor that keeps farmers from operating commercially is the economic aspect.

Advances through Aquaponics and Other Systems

Aquaponics is the combination of hydroponic gardening and aquaculture, fish farming. Aquaponics is an efficient and sustainable food production approach because there is no wastage: fish waste is fed into the hydroponics farm to feed the plants while the plants filter the water for the fish. Therefore, the water goes from the fish to the plants, and back in a perfect circle.

As the future dictates, taking up sustainable methods of food production is going to be critical, and aquaponics is a great way to go about it, for both small-scale and large-scale food production.

Interestingly though, other animals are being integrated into the sustainable methods of farming such as rabbits, worms, chicken and crickets, among others. As more people launch creative ideas into their farms, we expect more animals to become part of this unique biological hydroponic system.

Hydroponics in Grocery Stores and Restaurants

Other latest trends like this one, are not related to hydroponic growing, or the system, but on the application of the system. You must have seen that grocery stores and restaurants are now making hydroponic systems part of their business structures, as a way to provide their customers with the freshest produce.

For example, restaurants are running living salad bars that set apart their food from restaurants that store their produce in freezers and fridges. Customers can now enjoy a fresh meal right from the garden. This development has not only helped to boost interest in the customers, but it is also a financially sound idea because the cost of growing produce is lesser than that of purchasing it. There has also been an upcoming trend of growing plants on the rooftop and vertically, on the walls. All these developments are meant to increase food production in the urban setup.

Transitioning to the Organic Side

Majority of the nutrients and fertilizers used in hydroponics systems, both in small scale and large scale farms, are synthetically manufactured chemical compounds. Although these nutrients have been behind the success and popularity of hydroponics farming, they are not organic. This is contrary to the growing trend where people only want to eat organic foods. In addition, the runoff you get into the environment when you empty your nutrient reservoir can be quite damaging to the environment. Therefore, farmers are opting for organic fertilizers and shunning the chemical compounds. The nutrient-filled organic produce is quickly replacing the manufactured substances.

Increased Conservation and Sustainability Measures

The concept of conservation and sustainability of processes has been ongoing for a while now, across the world. Sectors are looking for ways to get into the bandwagon from the construction industry and its green buildings, and now to hydroponics farming, among other sectors. Since hydroponics requires significantly less water and fewer fertilizers, the wastage is not as dire as in other methods of agriculture.

Therefore, hydroponics reduces pollution to the environment, reducing the need to conduct expensive studies, and the need for containment and catchment, which happens with other forms of agriculture. This advantage allows hydroponics farmers to tell a good story about their trade, which is appealing to the environmentally conscious consumer.

Hydroponics as Part of the Home Décor

The fact that there are now green plants in places where they never were, such as in wall hangings, on countertops, on window panes, on the roofs, and in other areas, is placing plants in new territories enhancing the beauty of where they are placed.

People who only saw hydroponics gardening as belonging to a secret room somewhere, the backyard or in a greenhouse, are now seeing its use in new elegant living spaces as a piece of art. As you will see around the spaces you visit, artificial and cut flowers are quickly losing their place to live flowers, as people increasingly realize the benefits of hydroponics in the home décor craft or industry.

Hydroponics as The Means to Enhance Breathing Air

Many people introduce container plants in a room to help clean up the air. This is the traditional way of doing it, and it has a few drawbacks. One of them is that it would take you many plants to make any significant difference because soil-grown plants are limited in their growth, which in turn limits their rate of carbon dioxide for oxygen exchange. Also, the plants can only have an effect on the little air that is around them.

However, once you install hydroponic plants into a building, you also introduce an air filter that combines the natural ability of many plants to cleanse the air, and the benefits of a fan, which overcome the limitations of soil-grown plants.

The fan gets in the air through the hydroponic system much faster than natural processes would, and once it is incorporated into the nutrient solution, it speeds up the plant's respiration, which in turn speeds up the plant's intake of carbon dioxide, and its growth rate. The growing medium also acts as an extra air filter. The result of this process is that the particulate and formaldehyde removal rate is faster, at least 1000% better than if you were to depend on the plants alone.

The Hydroponics Carnival Ride

For a serious gardener working with a small indoor space, making the most of the available space would mean growing your crops in several layers, providing each with its own grow lights, and a watering system. This requires a lot of money, causing many growers to give up and pull out of the business.

A garden in America, however, found the solution to working with small spaces. The owners found a way to save on the lighting and the nutrients solution too. They came up with a device that resembles a Ferris wheel, one large enough to hold about 80 plants, with its trays arrayed around an axis placed at the center. Rockwool or some similar medium is used to hold the plants in place, and only one light is placed along the axis, and it provides all the light the plants need for their development.

In comparison to the regular hydroponics setup, this new arrangement causes three times as much plant growth for every watt. The plants also get to pass through the trough containing the hydroponics nutrient solution to pick the nutrients they need for each 45 minutes cycle.

Growing Marijuana

Different parts of the United States are increasingly legalizing adult use of marijuana, and in the process, creating a standardized regulated market for the product. Marijuana is used for both recreational and medicinal use, and its market is quite huge across the world. Regardless of the individual reservations, some people have regarding the industry; we have to admit that big business and many opportunities are lying in this industry, that farmers can take up.

As you would expect, the infant marijuana industries have established some stringent regulations, similar to those we see in the production of food items. In addition, the consumption trends you see in food preferences among consumers are similar to those expressed by marijuana consumers: they want to ensure that what they are putting in their bodies is clean, does not contain any pesticides, and ideally, it was grown in an environmentally conservent environment.

Hydroponic systems make it easier to grow clean, chemical free, and quality marijuana. Farmers are able to respond to the plants' nutritional needs, and the result is that the produce is more, and its quality is superior to regularly grown marijuana. The farmers are able to stick to the standards set by the regulatory board, and they even meet the needs of the end user.

For farmers who think that the establishment of a regulatory board would make their farming much more difficult, hydroponics gardening would make their work easier. You will stay on the right side of the law without even knowing it. This is because hydroponics gardening only allows you to provide your plants with only that which is necessary, and stay away from chemicals that would have contaminants. You also do not have to apply pest and disease control chemicals because the hydroponics environment is clean and free of disease-causing pathogens. Pests do not get in there either.

Into the Future

As time goes by, we can expect to see many other radical technologies come up in hydroponic farming. For example, the solar panels we covered earlier is quickly being taken up, particularly in the aquaponic setup that seeks to capitalize on the self-sufficiency of the system. We are bound to see more homes taking up this technology because it will not only offset electricity costs related to hydroponics; households can also rely on it for various functions.

The idea of fiber optic solar connection systems is still in its infancy, but once it advances and turns into a practical power solution, it promises to be another development that will revolutionize hydroponics gardening and other forms of indoor production.

In summary

In this information age, people are increasingly aware that they are what they eat. Their health, their outward looks, and other functions of the body are all related to the diet. This knowledge has increased the demand for clean, fresh food in the markets and eateries, which has made hydroponics the perfect solution for feeding the fresh food demand in the dense urban areas.

In the next few years, we are sure to see hydroponic gardens popping up on the walls of buildings, on the rooftops, in people's kitchens, backyards, and other spaces. In addition, commercial farmers are taking up the hydroponic gardening idea to increase their production potential. Therefore, as we step into the future, we can be sure that food will not be an issue of concern, even as the world population increases, because hydroponics farming has proven to be an excellent antidote to issues of food and its availability.

You too could take matters into your hands and begin to produce healthy foods for your family, friends, or even as a way to make some extra money. You could set up some form of a home garden, even when living in an apartment. Place your plants on a countertop, or at the kitchen window, and you will be surprised that you can actually grow something good out of your small unused spaces. As you and others around you adopt this practice, hydroponics gardening is sure to become a major part of producing food, across the world.

As of 2018, the global hydroponics market was worth $23.94 billion, and in the period between 2019 and 2024, there's expected to be a 6.8% increase. Governments and non-governmental organizations are championing it due to the benefit of ensuring food security. While the costs of setup are currently high, the farmers continue to reap big profits. We expect that advancing technology will resolve the issues of costs, and when this happens, farmers will benefit greatly. Big companies are moving in to take advantage of the new big business, and you too deserve a piece of the action.

CONCLUSION

Thanks for making it through to the end of *Hydroponics: Beginner's Guide to Quickly Start Growing Your Own Vegetables, Fruits, & Herbs, and Learn How to Build Your Own Hydroponics Home Gardening System*. Let's hope it was informative and able to provide you with all of the tools you need to achieve your goals whatever it is that they may be. It would be impossible to exhaust all there is to hydroponics farming, but the author sampled the most important bits of information to help you understand, possibly rouse your interest, and get you moving into the world of hydroponics.

Our world is changing in all kinds of aspects. The population is increasing steadily, the land that we have been farming for centuries is becoming poorer, and the farming spaces are becoming smaller as people build houses and infrastructure. While the resources continue to shrink, our population is demanding more cleaner food, and science has come up with one of the most genius ideas: hydroponics. Without requiring any soil to grow plants, anyone can now take up farming, wherever he or she is, whatever space is available. Everyone can now get in on the move that seeks to ensure that we will be able to produce enough food for ourselves in the coming days.

Now that you have gathered all these important facts, the next step is to go ahead and put into practice. Teach others around you the basics of hydroponics farming, and possibly, the move towards self-sustainability will ensure that there are enough affordable, clean and healthy people for the people in our societies, in and out of season.

Finally, if you found this book useful in any way, a review on Amazon is always appreciated!

DESCRIPTION

It is always a good thing to get in on the action and participate in what has been tested and proven good for the society, such as hydroponics gardening, but it is even more profitable when you go into it with your eyes open. Some people will want to try out hydroponics just because they saw someone doing it, and they perceive it to be an easy thing to do. However, as fun and interesting as hydroponics may seem, it is challenging and needs to be taken up only by informed minds.

To that end, the author has arranged all relevant information on hydroponics into chapters that will let you in on all there is with hydroponics. You will get the proper definition of hydroponics, how it works, the tools you need to work it, and various hydroponics systems from which you can choose. You will also be informed of the benefits you stand to enjoy and the disadvantages you have to endure when you choose hydroponics. Nevertheless, this is one of the most profitable and practical ways to grow crops as we step into the future with a large health-conscious population who are all about the quality and not the quantity of food.

Going by popularity, you can already tell that hydroponics farming brings many benefits. It shortens the growth span of crops, increases the quality of produce and heightens the quantity of food produced. Hydroponics is also being taken up for its aesthetic value, to clean up the air indoors, and as a way to reduce environmental pollution due to the use of less water and fertilizers.

What's more, manufacturers are now starting to produce organic hydroponic fertilizers, which means that farmers will not only be enjoying the returns from selling their vegetables, they will also have a great story to tell about environmental conservation.

Every piece of information you would need as you get into this increasingly popular method of farming you will see in this book. Kindly take note of the common mistakes beginners make in hydroponics gardening, and take measures to avoid falling into those pitfalls. This way, you will avoid making the mistakes others have made, and therefore avoid suffering the devastating losses that they suffered.

Inside this book you will find:

- The most explicit description of hydroponics
- The most vivid explanation about how hydroponics work
- The most exhaustive list of crops for which hydroponics farming is best suited
- An extensive list of tools and equipment you will need for your hydroponics garden
- The most useful tips to get you through the business seamlessly
- A list of common mistakes hydroponics beginners make, and how to avoid them
- The most precise directions to guide you as you start your first hydroponics garden
- The most accurate prediction of the future of hydroponics farming, and how you need to position yourself to receive all the benefits there will be.